Froggie: The Lost Waif

Froggie: The Lost Waif

Joseph Reyna de Barrios
Josephine Reyna de Barrios
Maria F. Davis

iUniverse, Inc.
New York Lincoln Shanghai

Froggie: The Lost Waif

iUniverse, Inc.

For information address:
iUniverse, Inc.
2021 Pine Lake Road, Suite 100
Lincoln, NE 68512
www.iuniverse.com

This is a very true story with actual names, dates and places.

Book design by Maria F. Davis

ISBN: 0-595-31341-8

Printed in the United States of America

Dedicated to
America, a grateful thank-you for accepting me.
England, very much obliged for discarding me.
Those, who spent their lives for others.
"Lest We Forget."

Froggie

Contents

INTRODUCTION

Although this true story begins in April of 1904, its genesis has the taproot into deeply hidden sources before this date. Ransom is generally the anticipated purpose for a kidnapping but not this time. What rewards could be wanted? Who commits the kidnapping? How many conspirators are involved? Most importantly is, why does it happen? It will take years of detainment and WW I with many cover-ups before this captive learns any of the truths.

The goal of the story is to share with the reader the valuable substance of hope along with the inhumane criminalities that some men achieve. The presence or absence of hope or cruelty can determine one's outlook on life. At times hope appears in abundance. Other times it is depleted. These ups and downs leave indelibly honest checkmarks in a private corner of the mind. Acts of cruelty can remain as vivid as when it happened or altered to be less severe in order to negotiate the continuance with life.

Froggie tells his story his way because then can we readily see the difference of a war between countries armed with fighting power and a war of elite authorities armed with official power. He reveals how his experiences mold him into the man he becomes but also points to persons in high places lacking the basic traits of compassion besides conscience. Bear in mind that being victimized for so long and throughout his malleable years, this brave child could have easily taken other roads to follow.

By happenstance a boy is abducted. His picture fills the newspapers. The long journey has taken him across several continents. One night in 1904, he finally is brought to a fortress in England. The tall friendless buildings seclude him. Alone and frightened, he does not know what is going to happen. He cannot understand his kidnappers. He only speaks Spanish. They don't.

Brought to a utilitarian type room, the child is interrogated. Because of the late hour and his exhaustion from lengthy travel and the language barrier and his fear of these strangers, the child is unable to give these four men the information they undoubtedly desire. Roughly handled, ending with several hard cuffs to his head by one of the well-dressed strangers, that lands him across the drafty floor, the child is finally left alone. Still dazed, with pain making itself known in both eyes and a sudden inability to focus, the small child curls up where he is, covering his bare knees with the hem of his new woolen sailor coat his Madre had tailors make for him. He buries his face into his chest, fearing that his cries might bring back *los hombres terrible*.

Early morning he awakens with the urgent call of nature but he dares not to move. When will the big train bring his Mother and Nanny to him? But no one comes for him, that day or ever again. When the door opens he goes with the girl who motions to him. She is very thin and unhappy looking. No smile crosses her lips. The hand taking his is bony leather. He is unaware that he is to be indoctrinated to a new way of life from this day, hereafter.

Overworked and most often, past his endurance, each day Froggie copes with his dreadful loneliness yet the ordeal for survival remains strong. He falls into the habit of sorting the people he sees; "them" from "us," while being patiently vigil to find release.

Years creep along with many more superiors to serve before he meets the one unlikely person who becomes his crusader and wife. The Brooklyn born would-be Catholic nun, "gentle" Josie, prefers to stay in the background yet I am determined to bring her to the reader's notice; out of love for being my precious Mama, for devoting her life to her husband's quest and to not give in when adversities keep coming to strike us and my equally precious Daddy who would give up his search to protect those he loves, only we would not let him.

I am certain that because of my mother's unwavering tenacity she was able to extract truths or assistances from consuls, Ellis Island immigration agents, His Majesty's Navy, Britain's War Office, the French Convent Superior Mother, Canadian Customs agents, Head Master of Dover Orphanage, Guatemalan journalists, British and American Police, West Point Military Academy, United Fruit Company and so many others.

There would be no pot of gold at the end of their search but the prize remains priceless to us, today and always. Truth. Too bad things happen that have to be hidden. The effort for concealment is more costly than the original deed, as some officials in high places must have learned. Yet, because of these happenings, this couple has left their Ethical Will.

In case you wonder why it took so long to deliver this book in print, know that I am guilty for much of the delay. Froggie would either write out the passages long-hand or dictate some parts to "gentle" Josie who would sit at her ancient Royal (with many worn keys) having to double check and re-check words and phrases unfamiliar to her. They finished most of what they started before traveling on in the mid-eighties. Afterwards, I couldn't come to terms with my losses and I would swell with too much emotion just to finish with transferring the manuscript to electronic means. Having completed this difficult goal; adding my own few words and editing everything, I am bound by family tradition to complete my end of the project. There's more to this story that will be told at another time, between other book covers. M.F. Davis

1

The Workhouse

The first permanent residence that I can remember was the largest house in the town but not the biggest structure by any means, although it is maintained and supervised very much like the military installations, which were in a Garrison Port nearest the continent of Europe. There were no direct connections between these different barracks and my new home but the Workhouse had routines for boys that were similar to the soldiers with one very big exception-there was no furlough for service rendered, with no promotions or privileges.

Now it is time to ponder why a young boy expensively dressed, who cannot speak a word of the English language, is admitted to the Poorhouse in Dover, England, in the month of April, in the year, 1904?

Because of my language difference I am not put with the numerous children who are already there. Instead, the Infirmary is to be my new abode. The Infirmary is one section of this establishment that is sprawled upon the side of a hill in the far end of the town, at the very end of Union Road.

Dover Union housed many inmates in their various departments; from the cradle to the grave. The male and female infirmaries overlook the entire place. Directly below them are the able-bodied men and women, separated, in order to be proper. The old men and women are treated in like manner, of course. Also, there are the nursery, the boys' and girls' quarters, a large kitchen and laundry where the able-bodied men and women work together.

Often I had seen opposite sexes folding sheets but at the time there was no way that I could attach any importance to that. However, during my eleven years of incarceration at least three boys and one girl were born to a married couple that worked in the laundry. There are no special quarters provided for them. They worked on sheets and had no intention of trying to make a living in the outside world. Certainly they could not keep their children there long because John Bull (a typical Englishman) would take them for cannon fodder.

Restrictions prevented my ever seeing the inside working conditions of any other department except when I was fortunate enough to be hospitalized on a few occasions. In order to get that privilege one had to be very sick or badly injured.

For five days in the week a doctor would visit the Poorhouse at noon and while away the time for which he was contracted. On his first visit following my being committed, he vaccinated me. I remember well, standing in front of an open fire watching the rain trickling down the window. *O to be in England* to get four sores put on my left arm in the shape of a Y. Upon being introduced to him I acquired the name, Frenchy, although I could not speak or understand that language, either.

The Supervisor of the Infirmaries kept me with her until I learned the language then I was placed in the girls' department because I was considered an infant. Parting from her hurt me deeply and well I remember her. Miss Foster was a gracious lady, tall, fair complexion with pure white hair. An appropriate name, I believe, for one who bestowed so much affection on me to the point where she was requested to resign shortly after our separation. During my stay with her I had made a friend with a young woman in the Infirmary, whom according to my recollection, had nothing more wrong with her than a constant twitching of the head. She was transported to a mental institution in another town. Her name was Jane Bowls.

Could it be that Miss Foster had to leave because of doing something that was regarded as an infraction of the rules; by arranging with the Supervisor of the girls to have me passed through a dining room window and sneak up the back way to have a Sunday dinner with my benefactor? That treatment was exceptional for one lone pauper child among one hundred fifty or more but being so young, that did not enter my head. Nevertheless, I was overjoyed for a short time, then on a given signal I returned in the same way. The same window was opened for my return. The Master of the boys waiting to gather me to him, he would close the window and hurry me back among the girls. So three staff members had jeopardized their positions for me, who, up until this time speculated that I had either been unwanted, too hot to handle or forcibly taken from my one or more parents and relatives.

If the latter was the case, where were they? Alone and broken hearted like me when I was separated from Miss Foster? I must have felt the same then but time had done its healing. Before my commitment to Dover Union I recall being with a woman on a horse-drawn street-car. When the end of the line was reached I insisted on staying to watch the horse being turned around. On another occasion there was a place where a woman was washing clothes outside, in a kneeling position. Close by was a large barrel of water into which I fell while playing. I later remembered the man who brought me to this Paupers' Palace in a hansom cab and stopping at a confectionery shop to buy something for me.

That now is in the past. The last visible friend had gone but there was someone, somewhere, who ordered a shoemaker to measure me for shoes to match the expensive clothes that I wore on Sunday. Also, a large rocking horse was given to me-different from the one that was already there and mine was more expensive.

Apparently, it is assumed that I was unable to care for myself because a girl of thirteen years is assigned to care for me. She washes my head, hands and knees twice daily. She escorts all the infant boys to bed at six o'clock, into a separate dormitory. A chore she does with enthusiasm combined with a heavy hand. She is very thin. When she boxes your ears for not doing her bidding those bony hands leave an impression on your memory. That is the technique she uses to remind us that she is a maiden among boys. After having instilled fear into me she then takes a liking for me. Nightly, after making each child close his eyes, she would then lay beside me. Ofttimes have I wondered if the poet who wrote, *O To Be In England Now That April's Here,* meant it. That ordeal which I endured was a punishment for those who enter this country at that time of the year.

With the tolling of a large bell at five forty-five each morning, the whole institution is aroused including the youngest children regardless of their physical conditions. The rules are to be observed in that every individual has to get out of bed. The only exceptions are for the bed patients in the Infirmaries. The daily routine is for all the children to get dressed, then line up in the middle of the dormitory with their shoes in their hands, next to be marched downstairs by command to the washroom where everyone strips to the waist. Our heads are put into a bowl of cold water and soaped all over with the all-purpose soap supplied for ablution and floor scrubbing.

The skinny one with bony hands works me over in that way each morning as though nothing has happened the night before. Or it could be that she was disappointed because there was a distinct lack of tenderness towards me whereas in the evening wash-time she seems to be pleasant. To notice this at that time in my life, could it be that I was not an infant in the legal sense of the word?

During this time I am not attending school, as I have to spend the days with those who are under six years of age, confined to a room with bare wooden floors. A fourteen-year-old girl having completed her schooling, watches over us. She has the title of Trainer but actually she is a trainee. She, having reached that age with at least three years of experience at scrubbing floors on hands and knees with Sundays off, treating stone and tile floors in a similar manner, cleaning porcelain, polishing brass with crude materials, working in the staff kitchen, beginning and ending each day by being a wet nurse to four children, is finished with her formal schooling.

She is nothing more than a child herself yet it is her day's routine between five forty-five in the morning and eight o'clock in the evening. Girls like this; being overworked and very much underfed, are trained in this way. They are taught to be dutiful and reminded often that they should be thankful for the three meals each day, the roof over their heads and for their beds. She does not complain in the least about her lot. These reminders are constantly repeated so as to build her morale. When she excels in her work she will be placed with some upstart or snobbish family to show others that they could afford a maid. Generally, a girl with this background would become a *slave* for people living many miles away. To be alone, separated from her brother or sister, living with a fear that if she does something to displease her employers she would be sent back to the Poorhouse.

In the event that if the conditions are displeasing to her, she could not escape until she has different clothes. The wearing apparel given to her upon leaving the Paupers' Mansion is unique and outstanding to the point where one would not want to be seen so clothed. To further humiliate the wearer, each item of clothing is marked with an oval stamp, about three inches long with letters that are at least three-quarters of an inch, *Dover Union, Dover*. In case *Dover Union* stamp is not enough of a distinguishing mark it is also stamped, *Given Away Free*.

For this most generous act by the administrators of this reform school for orphans and children of unfortunate parents, it would be expected of this girl to write a letter of thanks to the Chairman of the Board of Guardians, who represents the taxpayers; each of whom acts as though he owns a piece of each child in the place.

Not to be forgotten, also, that with all the qualifications a girl like this would have to give her employer, such as being hard working, obedient, and efficient, but also pretty. Yet, never in the eleven years I am here did any person of means ever take a girl; one who was so worthy of a good start to face the world. All those of us who have been educated to be honest, trustworthy and confirmed in the church of the country, are without having any voice in the matter regardless of their parents' religion. Once inside these walls everybody joined the Church of England. It is the wealthy that generally go bargain-hunting yet children like us are not given the advantages of their bounty. This is to be expected in a country that has first, second and third class coaches on its railways.

A girl who was rigidly taught to respect authority would be placed in a cheap boardinghouse to be used and probably abused until she reaches the age of twenty-one or that a prince charming comes to her rescue by marrying her. Boardinghouse slaves. Such has to be the fate of a number of these girls, especially orphans from the Workhouse.

2

Lost Waif Goes To School

According to rule, if one is too young to attend school he is confined to the day-room. Not to play but to sit rigidly on a bench until school is dismissed. Now the time has come for me to join that select group. I have looked forward to that day because it would give me the opportunity to see what it is like on the outside and some measure of freedom.

Whereas, inside these walls we are required upon rising each morning to march from the dormitories to the washroom, from there to the dining hall and march out following each meal. On days without school or classes we must make formation and march six times daily. On Sundays we also make formation and march to and from the chapel. Now school means an additional four times with a half-mile walk each way. By our doing this we become objects of curiosity; infants gape, brats sneer and throw barbs and dogs bark as this company of about sixty girls with a dozen infant boys parade through the streets. The supervision of this regimented body is not done by a paid member of the staff but by the oldest girl. All are uniformly attired with boyish hair-cuts on girls under twelve years of age. The older ones have their hair tied at the back of the neck with black tape. The boys are shorn.

In weather fair and foul, in sickness and in health, everyone goes to school marching on the sidewalks; a courtesy shown by the generous tax-payers towards the female regiment. But if one among us happens to be sick, a little matter like that could wait until the noon recess regardless of how serious the malady might be.

At last I enter my first classroom. It is terraced and each pupil has a desk with an attached seat, with mine being close to a wall where directly above me is a picture of a robin. To many, this may not seem unusual but this is the first framed picture I have seen since leaving the infirmary. There are times that I imagine the bird moves, to the extent that it distracts me from being attentive to the teacher.

Needless to say, the robin and I have to be separated after having kept company for a short while. I am sent to another class in a room adjoining.

Upon entering this room, the teacher must have thought that I am old enough to know my full name. When she asks for it to write in the class register, I answer, "Frenchy is my name," as I have been called nothing else. This is how it is from the first day in school when the teacher calls the roll at the beginning of each half day. Whereas the other children answer, "Present" to two names, such as, "Tommy Jones," I am the lone one called "Frenchy." When the news is spread around the school the name gets changed slightly to, "Froggie," and that is the name I become known by to all the kids.

In that room there are no pictures on any of the walls. In fact, according to my recollection, the room is dismal in regard to light, as no sunshine comes into it. Fortunately, my stay in that class is not for long, as I am sent to another class. This room is different, filled with girls and plenty of daylight streaming through large windows. It is a girls' school with two rooms for children of each sex, from the age of six to seven years. I had passed through each class only to find myself alone. I am one lone boy in a class of all girls. It does not seem strange to me in the least because all my time was being spent with girls; marching, eating, playing and even going to sleep with one.

The teacher of this class is a lovely person. She is young and pretty with beautiful golden hair. To this day I still remember her name. My first lesson being taught by her-how to write the letter "S", capital and small, with a pen dipped in an inkwell. This may seem insignificant but how long does one stay as an infant? Until this time I had no name other than the single one before mentioned. Who does know my name or from whence I came? Maybe there is some uncertainty as to my sex?

Day follows day of the same monotonous disciplined routine until at long last my infancy terminates and I am placed with all boys. Everything is much the same with a few minor exceptions. The distance to the boys' school is half a mile farther. Going there, the boys march under the supervision of an inmate but not on the sidewalk-not daring to obstruct the paths of taxpayers. The scenery changes slightly; passing more pubs and shops, also marching parallel to the tracks of tram-cars.

It is a bright sunny day: this, my first in a different school. On arriving I am taken to the Headmaster, whereupon, a note is given to him by the one in charge of marching us. Following next, I am given a name with a handle attached. This ends the use of "Frenchy" by the teachers.

The monicker pinned on me is typically British in that it coincides with the name of a street in London. It is the beginning of my being manufactured into an Englishman; as it is extremely doubtful that I am born one. However, there is nothing I could do to change these conditions because having learned from the experiences of others: that crying, screaming and the showing of temper would not bring about freedom such as these boys enjoyed, whom I have now joined to sit in the class.

The room is void of any kind of decoration except for the variety of clothes on the backs of these kids on the outside. Such is the term that we use for the ones who are not going through an indeterminate period of incarceration in the Workhouse. This school matches it with its bare red brick walls ands wooden floors. It is the beginning of a seven-year-stretch in a school that has two rooms. One room is divided into three sections by one large curtain and one sliding partition. There are just four teachers and one Schoolmaster. He teaches the seventh grade. One teacher teaches all the subjects in the first and second grades. Another teacher teaches all subjects in the third and fourth grades but these grades are divided by a narrow aisle. The same set-up goes for the fifth and sixth grades. Undoubtedly, it makes for a cheap education.

The ways we are disciplined and taught are most effective. For these reasons I am grateful, as it is far better to have received an efficient education rather than a quality education that costs so much more and produces less results.

For instance, we are taught decimals in the third grade; long division and multiplication, ratio and percentages in the fourth grade; algebra equations and square roots in the fifth and sixth grades; with geometry in the seventh grade. Add to this the numerous tests in mental arithmetic and the learning of music without an instrument (except for a tuning fork) with notes chalked on a blackboard. We are taught all the simple marching songs of the Navy and of different regiments: *The Minstrel Boy To The War Has Gone, In The Ranks Of Death You'll Find Him,* and *Annie Laurie,* for whom one would lay down and die. Add to the music this kind of poem: *Half A League Onward Into The Valley of Death Rode The Six Hundred,* written by Lord Alfred Tennyson. Then there are the ones about himself when he gets ready to "kick his bucket": *Crossing The Bar* or *The Funeral of Sir Thomas Moore* (when not a funeral note was sounded) and *The Slave's Dream.* These songs and poems matched our way of life.

Did these supposedly great personages get their titles for writing such morbid stuff just to brainwash kids into giving themselves in later years to be killed needlessly? Another phase of such education-*to lead us into the valley of death*-is the lesson each class has to hear at separate times and which is drilled into us on the average of once a week. When one has the lesson forty-five times a year for seven years (standard operational procedure for all schools throughout the country) upon entering the Armed Forces. It comes as no surprise to me that the training begins with a rifle.

At that time in my life there was a reason for this training because the country had a history for going to different parts of the world to start wars. The truth will never be known. Reported news was more often nothing but propaganda. According to law, history is a compulsory subject in school. How many centuries of the stuff has to be pushed into the heads of pupils, to do nothing more for them than to detract from one's thinking power?

Another part of education that may be considered as quality is to learn to recite some of Shakespeare. The gruesome parts such as the, *Princes in the Tower* (to have their eyes burnt) and the *Merchant of Venice* (where one is to give a pound of flesh without the loss of one's blood) have certainly kept me in good stead during my life's adversities. Another subject reminiscent of gore to me is geography; with its books on the subject and with maps of all the countries where Britain had the Empire coloured in red.

The school day began in the same way; with the sliding partition being pushed back (the curtains, also) with the first graders coming into the larger room. Then began the first lesson that all pupils could join in collectively; in order to develop the mind, conscience and soul but it was neither the salute to the country's flag nor the singing of the national anthem. In their stead we said, *The Lord's Prayer* and sang a hymn that was selected by a class that was its favorite.

I was in the fourth grade when that class selected, *O Happy Band Of Pilgrims*. Being a member of a band of pilgrim paupers, it was not my choice. I did enjoy taking part in its rendition when the turn came. What a beautiful way to start a day by hearing a couple hundred of boys' voices singing in harmony. It is known to us that others enjoyed our singing. They are the people living in the houses that surround the school.

Then in 1914, while the school closed for the month of August, a change had been made in these houses. Instead of the occupants who were tenants (being the only ones to hear us sing and say our first lesson) a regiment of troops had been added to our audience.

It is this country's Declaration of War on the fourth of that month. Each morning at the same time we assemble in the schoolyard in formation. A bugle would be blown on the street for this undressed, non-uniformed regiment to fall in line. Immediately, front doors fly open. Up from basements or down the steps come the six hundred, more or less, to make formation on the street.

They are the pick of the nation's young men. A robust Sergeant Major bellows commands until we begin our morning prayer. Then silence seems to befall on the world for these brief moments until the end of the hymn. Then the commands are renewed for this troop to obey and it is well done. It is an impressive sight to see these young men. Some have wooden rifles for drill purposes only, with more being added daily. Some have parts of military uniforms, khaki tunics here and there that mingle with the blue ones of the militia. The remainder of the militia would be wearing mufti.

They are smart in their drill. There is evidence enough to show that part of their education has not been forgotten. These men have answered the call to arms to such an extent that there is not room at the military installations. They are billeted with families on orders, not by choice.

The school year ends in December. This year in particular is the termination of my formal education. In the seven years spent at that school I have passed through all the grades in an unusual way. While in the first grade that began in the summer of 1907, the Schoolmaster would single me out occasionally to spend recess with him to do writing exercises. Promotion did not come for me in the usual way, such as at the end of each year. Instead, while the schoolmaster is teaching class, I am singled out and taken to the next class. That happened in the second year in the first grade. I am placed in the third grade during my second year then transferred to the second grade in my third year and then promoted to the fourth grade. I spend one full year in the fourth grade then two years in the fifth grade. Whereas boys with lower marks than mine are elevated. I could not understand why this was happening to me. I inquired. No reason was given to me for my being left back. But I did not further question the issue, more so from fear than anything else. Then after doing one half term in the sixth grade, promotion came to me alone. The rest of the time was spent in the seventh grade. Was I just marking time? Why?

During those seven years I did well in arithmetic and shown an interest in geography. But history with its grim tales of beheading a woman, the long red line of Crimea, the Black Hole of Calcutta and the colonization of Australasia, were not adventurous stories to me with appeal to cultivate one's brain. However, there is one phase of this subject matter, which was taught to us by the schoolmaster. When he was required to take the upper classes, his teaching was about the balance of power and that was worth remembering.

On this matter he would describe how the balance of power originated in the Eastern part of the world and had moved westward until it had come to this country, saying, "but it will not stay here, although you sing, *Brittania Rules The*

Waves and the country can muster a large army for its Empire," he did say. It was his prediction that the balance of power would go westward and stay in a young country, one that was nearest to being self-supporting.

"America is the nation of the future," was his reference, "The first and only colony to sever itself from the Crown." Instructions of this nature had taken place before the First World War. If any boys who were in the classes took this genuine propaganda home to their parents, they also must have been in accord because not one person came to challenge these remarks or to call him anti-British.

During my school years a change had been made in our march to school routine, due to a slight accident sustained by one of our boys. This boy was nine years old and had feet that compared with the position of the hands on a clock when the time is two-forty-five. One day while marching on our customary track in the gutter, a tram-car was overtaking us at the same time a horse-drawn cart with bags of coal was passing. The cart's wheels ran over his toes. There was no stopping for an incident like this. We older boys at the rear of the Paupers' Brigade took turns in carrying him pick-a-back the rest of the way. For the first time in ten years we marched out of step with a crying boy on one of our backs. There was no telephone in the school. The schoolmaster did know that there was an infirmary in the Workhouse yet the boy had to suffer until we carried him back at the end of the day. Fortunately, it was only for three hours, as it happened prior to the afternoon session. His shoe was not removed to check his condition until a nurse did it when we got him back to the Almshouse. It was found that the tips of two toes were smashed.

From that time on we were given the privilege of going to school free-style. We went in a group just the same because of the hostile attitude of the people only too eager to report us, should they consider that one of us had stepped out of line (especially when we passed one shoe repair shop). This proprietor was always at the front of the store, seated at his workbench. Although no one ever told us but due to the resemblance, we knew that he was the brother of the headmaster over us in the Poorhouse. Therefore, if a boy got a good spanking while in bed, we knew that he had been reported by this snobbye (the name given to shoemakers).

He did not know us by our names but he would ask one boy the name of another. Although we had a code of ethics, we could not suppress the information because he would come and pick us out of the line-up. We did not deface or damage property. The only offense committed would be a little horseplay by one who forgot about the shoemaker sitting in the window.

In order to avoid confrontations with the boys on the outside, we Union boys left the school at the end of each session, five minutes prior to classes being dismissed. Before that rule was introduced, fights amongst us were common occurrences, not as gangs but one on one, because of the verbal abuse to which we were subjected. These incidences would be presented to the headmaster but only we juvenile paupers were punished with getting three cuts of the cane on each hand. Therefore, the change in the quitting time helped us.

In the event that we bore marks of violence, such as a black eye or a nosebleed, we got it again from the headmaster with a good slapping of the face and extra work. Also, we were made to stand in the corridor with face to the wall and hands at arm's length above the head. The infraction carried this penalty for one week and in receiving it, one needed keen hearing for the simple reason that it is only natural for one to tire and slump. Then stealthily, the headmaster, upon seeing this dereliction of duty, would attack from behind with a barehanded smack on the ears. The shock was worse than the blow. By the same token the person who delivered the blows must have thought that his military training was for such purpose. It was always an ex-army man who supervised, in order to develop us into first-class cannon fodder.

Now that my school days are over it is time to relate through that period of time in the Workhouse. Such is the term used to define the department of the institution and not the team of any sport. Boys between the ages of seven and nine inclusive, were seven o'clockers; meaning that they went to bed at that time of day. Before doing so the final chore had to be done, such as rolling down stockings, stripping bare to the waist, immersing the head into a wash-basin of cold water and lathering that part of the person with an all-purpose piece of dark brown soap followed by the washing of the knees.

There was no heat in the room although it got quite cold many times. There was no relaxing of the rules. So with shivering bodies and chattering teeth that had not as yet been introduced to a brush, it was off with the boots in hand and to march off to bed. Each dormitory had thirty-six beds where each boy had to undress, fold his clothes neatly then get into a nightshirt where the temperature was no higher than all the other rooms.

Before jumping into bed on orders and under supervision, all had to kneel beside their beds, close eyes, clasp the hands together and say prayers. If any words were uttered they were cut short, as we would still be shivering. Except for change in sex, an older boy whose hand was much heavier was now doing this overseeing. Otherwise, the procedures and the end results were similar to those experienced as an infant but with one difference. He kept walking until all were asleep.

3

On The Boys' Side

Occasionally there would be nights when no one could go to sleep because of a new admission. On the first night of separation from his parent or parents (as was often the case) he would begin with a slight sniffle that gradually developed into a sobbing, then on to a broken-hearted cry accompanied by, "I want my mother." No effort was made to quiet him, as this behavior was commonplace with every admission whose age most of the time was under ten years. Although he was left to cry without interruption, we all knew that at ten o'clock it would be forcibly stopped. Why was this boy crying? We, who had been in this place so long as not to remember the parting of mother from son, knew also, that his living conditions with his mother must have been bad. In all probability, his father was in the infirmary with what was termed consumption, contracted as a diver in the construction of the Dover Harbour. While the one for whom the boy was crying, had been admitted to the women's department.

At precisely ten o'clock, the elderly inmate who assisted the master would retire to bed at the end of a row of eighteen beds and would not tolerate a crying child in the room. Without hesitation, he would go to the boy's bed and slap his bare buttocks until quiet reigned.

That same elderly inmate was an intellectually intelligent person who spent the last two hours of each day seated at a bellows organ playing minuets, waltzes and scottisches (Scottish tunes). He had been a schoolmaster in Northern County but had lost his wife while in that position. The tragedy was the reason of his resorting to strong drink, causing the ending of his days with us. He was tall and slender with a long white beard. We never knew his age.

After knowing him ten years, he remained the same as when I first met him. He certainly knew how to deal with boys. Because of this, he commanded our respect at all times and we liked him, too. His main purpose was to serve the food; cut the bread for the morning and evening meals; and ladle milk, tea, or coffee, depending on the day of the week. This is what we sang a hymn of thanks for; bread with margarine four times, bread with jam two times and bread with sugar two times each week while the remainder was bread with nothing.

Many times during my eleven years of imprisonment, the margarine would be rancid but there never was a complaint. The jam was something else. This came in seven-pound earthenware jars with a beautiful picture of all the fruits that grew in this Merry England. The factory where it was made was located quite close to the school we attended. Oft times we saw the ingredients for this delicacy being drawn by a horse pulling a cart filled with *mangold wurzels*, (special for paupers). But on two occasions in all that time there was an addition to the evening meal. We got some lettuce because too much had been grown for the staff by a new gardener.

The one outstanding mid-day meal was the one served on Monday consisting of cold boiled mutton, cold boiled rice (mush-like) and cold suet pudding. As hungry as we were this meal was not touched by anyone. For years it came and went the same way. By so doing, we were being taught hypocrisy due to our singing *thanks* for what was to be eaten, then sitting awhile just looking at the food, finally rising and singing words of our deepest appreciation for what we had (not) eaten.

After years of these Monday Specials, the headmaster of our internment camp decided to pay us a visit while we were entranced with what lay before us. He went to one boy and asked, "Why don't you eat that good food?"

With his meager knowledge of etiquette, the boy said, "It's rotten!" This was more than that. The food was unappetizing and unpalatable. So he was subjected to a severe reprimand and punishment for this uncouth reply but we could not share his penalty although he spoke for all of us. For all that, there was no change made in the meals. I often wondered if the same stuff was not saved for the following Monday. There was nothing of consequence for which one could be deprived. The punishment was always the same regardless of the offense, if any had been committed. But his was *not to reason why*, to steal a line from Lord Alfred.

How gratifying it must have been for the master of the boys to be able to sneak from behind and give a whack with his bare hand, for just relaxing a little, that any boy was bound to do. At least that boy was not asked to apologize. It was doubtful if an apology could be extracted from him. Regardless of how hard the sneak attack was delivered, we had educated ourselves not to make a sound because this would mean a follow-up attack to shut us up. Usually a lump on the forehead would appear as we got it from two directions; the hand and the wall.

Boys at school on the outside would ask how the bumps came to be. The answer was, "I ran into a wall." The majority of the outside boys despised us as much as the Union Master despised us. To prove the point, during my seven years of schooling not one Union boy was ever invited into the house of anyone of them. We had to pass nearly all of them on our return to the "Mansion Miserables."

When the war broke out it brought a change in the Tuesday noonday meal. Where we had been used to boiled ham it was now changed to canned corn beef, the same as that being served to the men in the trenches in France and commonly called "bully beef" by them.

Other changes that were made were brought about by age. When a boy reached the age of ten he discarded his knickers for long trousers and began a four year apprenticeship; learning how to be a skilled floor scrubber on hands and knees. At this new endeavor he would get practice for six days in the week. Can anyone imagine what a wonderful scrubber one can become after working at it for one thousand two hundred fifty-three days? Please, do not question the extra day because there had to be a leap year in that time.

Due to an accident I sustained while playing one Sunday evening (playing was against the rules both in Heaven and here on Earth, so we were told to believe) I was rendered unconscious by landing on my head and suffered a concussion requiring my being taken to the infirmary where I spent one week. So there were six days that were not served.

Beginning with Saturday, should you ever have the desire to learn the lost art of scrubbing bare wooden floors, directions will follow. Beginning with the dining-hall, twelve apprenticed paupers would be detailed. Three were to wash the breakfast dishes, three to polish the steel knives, forks and spoons (stainless had not yet been invented) with the dust from a yellow brick, with water and rags, while the rest of the boys scrubbed twenty-eight tables and the same number of benches; each about ten feet long. These would then be pushed to one end of the room. By that time the preliminaries would be completed, then it was time to hit the deck. Next, each one of the twelve boys would get a pail, soap (the same used for washing our hides), a stiff scrub-brush, a rag and a thin pad for a kneeler. With all the tools of the trade, the pails were filled with water from one tap only. A line was formed at one end of the room, water put on the floor with the rag, the brush soaped. One boy at a time would count to thirty while the actual scrubbing was being done. After two patches were done, the water had to be changed from a single hot water tap. No cheating could be done because if the water was not steaming then it had to be redrawn. This work was being done under supervision. At the same time there were six more boys in each of the dormitories doing likewise.

At precisely ten o'clock a work stoppage would be called and all the boys would have to muster into the yard to receive the weekly dose of Epsom salts and it was not to soak our tired feet.

Is there any better way to develop strong healthy boys whose futures lay in the hands of Generals and Admirals? After swiftly swallowing the Epsom salts it was back to the numerology. Corners were cut wherever possible with one thing in mind, to play soccer with rags tied to resemble a ball. That would be played for minutes before the noonday meal. Such was the recreation on a day with no school.

Following the floors being scrubbed, the tables were put back into place and dishes set out for the next meal at twelve o'clock. In the sleeping quarters the beds were repositioned and made ready for use.

Upon completion of lunch we would be taken for a route march on a dusty road for two hours. For personal reasons it was not advisable to stay out any longer. Every evening with the exception of Sunday, the dayroom was scrubbed along with the stone-floored utility room and the aisles between the dining-hall tables.

Not one penny of the taxpayers' money was spent on us for recreation yet we could play competitive games among ourselves such as that before-mentioned; cricket; with a handmade rag ball and a board for a bat. The wickets were chalked on a wall; rounders (a game somewhat like baseball, using the same improvised equipment; tip cat,(made from a piece of circular wood and half a broomstick); kites(made with cotton, thin sticks and newspaper stuck on with soap and spit); and jump-back or leap-frog.

There were times when some Union boys were chosen to play on the school football team against other teams in the town. The team's shirts, shorts, stockings, shoes and footballs were paid for by weekly contributions from the boys who attended. The Education System supplied no funds for sports' activities but they did supply persons with good teaching abilities.

The inside-boys (Mansion paupers) who played were envied by the outside-boys because it was impossible to obtain donations from the former. For that reason they felt that it should not be allowed. Whereas we, on the inside, also envied them because they got out of all the floor scrubbing and they left for the game at ten o'clock on Saturday mornings, missing their hearty drink. For our part they were envied with pride, to know that we, the under-privileged, were able to fill a need.

During this period of time a sort of voluntary regimentation movement was being promoted in the guise of making boys on the outside better citizens. This movement had to be tactfully different from the compulsory kind to which we (on the inside) were committed. The end results were for the same purposes although it was not put in that language. Basically, it is a very good method of regimentation and if practiced throughout the world by peoples of all ages there would never be war. There is an exception and to this end the motive may be questionable. Because it was founded by an Army General who put this (regimenting) idea into practice while serving in India and later in South Africa during the Boer War. At the conclusion of that war and until this movement was started, there does not seem to be any record of it having been used. If a priest or someone totally non-military had started this movement then its purpose would not warrant doubts.

At the same time there was an organization in operation that exploited boys from very poor families for the colonization of a part of land for the Empire. There were occasions when amongst us boys who had left school and who were waiting to be found jobs, that some would be sent to that place for a physical examination and two weeks of testing to qualify for exportation.

One year, four of us boys were candidates, only to return at the end of the testing because all had failed. They had failed because of lack of strength and stamina. In fact, during my seven-year-stretch with the boys, not one ever made it that applied there. At least it was a change for them but not one that they relished to return. Along this line a certain amount of time and expense could have been saved if only our visiting doctor had been informed as to the requirements expected of these underfed and overworked kids who were to be the future builders of an empire…for whom?

This same doctor had the quickest way of curing kids of supposed minor ailments such as toothache, sore throat and bed-wetting. I had to see him when a tooth ached so much and a girl complained of a sore throat. He displayed chivalry by asking her first what hurt her. She replied by stating that she was unable to swallow because it hurt to do so. He told the girl to open her mouth wide. At the same time he took his watch from his vest pocket by the thick black leather fob with silver on the end, and rammed it into the girl's mouth and said, "See, you can swallow." With that she was sent back with no further treatment needed. Then turning to me with, "Hello, Frenchy, no, it's now Froggie, I am told. No matter, you never looked French. What is your complaint?"

"Toothache," I replied. I knew the remedy from others who have availed themselves of his dental services. To resist meant that two from the able-bodied male section would be detailed to stand by for the treatment that I was about to receive for relief. On the other hand there was the reward of a penny if I chose to cooperate fully. I chose the latter and his bidding by sitting in the chair, gripping the arms of it tightly, at the same time opening my mouth wide. Then in went the forceps clasping the molar. With a twist and a pull it was out and I was off and away, with one penny richer.

Had I put up any resistance those two men would have held me and forced my mouth open or failing that, the doctor would give me a slap across my face and send me on my way. He did not want any part of his only one-hour duty time wasted. He had arranged that on a certain Saturday, nine bed-wetting boys would be put into beds in the infirmary ward for circumcision. He had four inmates to serve as restrainers. He cut, sometimes sutured, those kids in a very short time, without pain killing medications of any kind and allowed them to stay there for one week. When they returned they were still bed-wetters. Why had these operations been performed by a person who took the oath to relieve pain and suffering? He was not tall but very thin and callously impatient. We feared him, not respected or trusted him. He kept getting smaller in my eyes.

About a year later we were all issued toothbrushes with mugs bearing the alphabet and pictures to correspond with the articles. Amongst us there were two and a half alphabets. If a boy broke his "A" he would take another mug so that he had a receptacle for his toothbrush that bore his number, something the mugs did not have. The first issue of these items was the last. There were no replacements. Also, boys later admitted, following this bestowal of mugs, were not given any. However, they were not needed to any extent because we all knew the alphabet. One thing about the mugs was that they did not bounce when dropped on a stone tiled floor, so they were short lived. It was only an act on the part of the Board of Guardians to be publicized in the weekly local paper.

At no time was there ever any mention of incidents that occurred within the confines of this barracks-like fortress; such as births, deaths, contagious diseases, accidents or fires. Fortunately there were no fires while I resided there. It was not deemed necessary to have more than two fire-drills in eleven years. The authorities were not moved to take precautionary steps along that line; even after the first air-raid on England, when a lone *Taube* dropped a bomb on this town of Dover on Christmas Eve of 1914.

Each year there was an outbreak of mumps and measles. Those who contracted the former were just kept from going to school while the latter were put into isolation without any particular care. On one occasion a boy collapsed at the breakfast table. He had been running a high temperature and before the day was out he was delirious. He had begun the day in the usual manner yet we could see that he was sick. But under the watchful eyes of two paid staff members this was not observed because, *His was to do or die*. Later, we heard that he had diphtheria.

However, he recovered because where he was sent for treatment there were nurses, bless them, who seemed to be the only ones in the world who cared for the welfare of us kids when we were placed in their hands. Due to the poor pay that they received, the changes among them were many but they were experienced and kind. The place could have done without the callous bag of bones that just ran through the place six times weekly.

One day a boy slipped while playing and broke his left forearm two hours after the doctor had done his sprint. A nurse set it and it healed without complications. There was one nurse who had been there as long as I had been. Most of the time she worked night duty. For one reason she would kneel to say audible prayer in each of the twelve wards of the infirmary after the lights went out. In that beautiful woman was the first, *Rose of no man's land*. She was an angel of mercy who was requesting power from God to heal these forgotten people.

No charitable organization contributed anything at anytime. For them, (these forgotten people) some were in wheelchairs, not from birth defects but from job accidents. Compensation had not been initiated for the working class as of that period, so it was their individual misfortune.

When a boy was admitted he did not get a physical examination, therefore, there were some unusual characteristics with some who entered our confines. One boy, for instance, although only eleven years old, he had a large cataract on each of his eyes causing them to be constantly moving yet this condition did not exempt him from work.

Then also, there were the stammerers, two of whom were chronic cases. One could not speak with breath inside of him. In order to perform talking he would wait until his lungs were empty then say the words hurriedly.

Imagine, if you can, the feeling that came upon us when there was a change of Headmasters and he asked this boy a question. When not receiving an immediate reply, he brought his hand across the boy's face, demanding an answer.

The one standing beside him in the line said, "He can't speak fast, sir."

Turning to him the Headmaster said, "You talk too fast," so his hand contacted another face. Sometime later the Headmaster deemed it necessary to speak to the other boy with the similar affliction. This boy was unable to communicate verbally unless he raised his right leg, stuttering at the same time and he would finish with a hard stamp to the floor, resulting in his getting a big hand too, for not keeping still.

Eventually, the elderly inmate who assisted him, not knowing about these brutal incidents, informed him about the condition of these boys. How heroic he must have felt? This six-footer, a chief warrant officer from one of the elite Calvary regiments, to be able to punch kids around; the majority of whom were orphans not delinquents in a reformatory. Word leaked out from the girls' side that his wife also meted out brutal punishment.

Then came the Declaration of War. With it came the recall to colours. I will refrain from using profanity with great difficulty for *this* person who learned how not to be a man among men. Prior to leaving the Paupers' Mansion, however, he demanded paid assistants for both him and the Headmistress, his wife. Both were provided with assistants. Not to be outdone, the inmate assistant requested an aide, who was supplied. He was an ex-army man with a moustache he twisted and waxed with soap; the same soap we used on floors and our bodies.

However, these changes were brought about before the Declaration of War. Perhaps otherwise we would have had advanced military training but as it turned out we were not to know. The assistant master was a well built young man of twenty-three, five feet ten inches tall with a kind heart; who did not raise his hand to any one of us and that eliminated the sneak attacks on those doing punishment, when he was on duty alone. He knew better than any one of us what it was like to be kicked around. It was for that reason he was with us.

His previous job had been with his father who operated a horse farm and it was this young man's job to break them in, resulting in his having to sustain fractured knees and collar bones. There were times when he would run. Then there were other times when he would simply step down, causing a knee to give way and swell painfully. When this happened he always selected me to massage and lace a padded cap onto it; something he always had close by.

When the war came he was left in charge. There was no relaxing of the work routine. We were thankful that the master, who ruled with an iron hand by making contact with kids' faces, was gone. We cared not at all as to what had happened to him from that time on. But his wife stayed which did not seem to interest our young master. He did show interest in her assistant; a young woman of twenty who eight years before had been a resident here, not as a pauper but as the daughter of a staff member. Oh, what a change that period of time had wrought on her; from a pretty girl to a beautiful woman in every way; gentle with the little ones and friendly to the older ones in her care.

There had never been a shortage of boys who had left school and were waiting to be placed in work positions. There were times when as many as twelve boys spent the time working and had time for recreation. But the war had brought a sudden change of circumstances and jobs. If only jobs were found for them it would have made everything all worthwhile. With the change came our first casualty. This boy had been with us quite a few years having been admitted with three younger brothers, an older brother and a sister. His older brother was in the Royal Navy. Their father had died in the infirmary from tuberculosis contracted when working as a diver on the construction of the Dover Harbour and while their mother was working in a paper mill but was unable to support her large brood. The older brother had left the Paupers' Mansion just before the war broke out. In late September of that year a man came from Southwest England in search for a boy to serve an apprenticeship on a fishing smack. This chosen boy saw six weeks of life on the outside of the Work House after spending so much time on the inside. The fishing smack that was selected to be his home for four years struck a mine and sank with all hands (usually numbering four) on board. With his being admitted to our Paupers' Palace, his mother had to relinquish all claim to him since she was unable to provide for him. Therefore she was not informed of his premature trip to his doom.

At the end of that year another of his brothers finished his schooling. I did, too. We were the only ones left inside while all the rest went to school. The same work that was done by ten boys was now to be done by two. There was not a minute in the day for sitting other than at mealtimes. We washed dishes for one hundred fifty kids, set the tables, swept the dining-hall, polished the brass on every door and polished faucets on sixteen wash-stands. We washed the floors in the utility rooms. This chore was done after we had begun the day by making up nine beds, sweeping that part of the dormitory, dusting it, then lining up the beds with the rest in the room. Pillows and the turned down sheets all had to be in line while we waited for the inspection; standing at attention in the front of each boy's section. All this work was done before we received the hearty breakfast of a piece of bread and three quarters of a pint of milk. Some mornings a spoonful of sugar would be served. Then only a half pint of milk would be doled out with such a wonderful delicacy.

At the end of the first week with just two boys doing the work there came another change. The mother of the other boy came to claim him. She could now provide for his well-being, as she now had two sons in the Navy and a daughter working in the same mill. It dawned on me the moment I found myself alone, that I was expected to do or attempt to do as much as ten boys used to do. I could not possibly do two persons' work, let alone ten but at the same time knowing that I would be worked to the end of the day, regardless.

This was an experience unrelated to anything that had happened to me in the past because besides all the work, it came with complete isolation for about five hours each day of school. Alone in a big place with no one to talk to and I was just being trained to meet the rigors of the world outside, or better yet, the world beyond. It did not seem to concern my two Masters that I was alone or else, they did not care. It stood to reason that one could not do all the work that had been done in the past by more boys. The older boys who were attending school were ordered to hurry back upon leaving school, in order to assist in keeping the work schedule.

Another reason for there being a shortage of boy power was because two years prior, a notice had been placed in the local paper stating that eligible orphans could be placed in the homes of people interested in boarding them. They would be paid the enormous sum of five shillings a week for each boy taken. All that was required of getting a boy or two was for the boys to sit on benches. The gifts were lined up in front of the takers at a given time on Saturday afternoons. The reviewing was held at the main entrance and it was a case of first come, first served. The twelve and thirteen-year-old ones were the first to be grabbed. Not solely for love but as much for avarice. Boys of this age were eligible to sell newspapers before and after school each day while the girls of the same ages were experienced home-makers.

There was none amongst them that was more eligible than I to be boarded out: my having no identity whatsoever, yet I was not permitted to enter into the parade. If at the time I had a relative anywhere, none could possibly know how to contact me. I came to this Heartbreak House without even knowing the language. Then who could I be? Those who had become attached to me had always left. Even unto the Headmaster and his assistant of the Union who were there when I was committed but with whom there were no attachments.

The boys who were not accepted at the first sale questioned me as to the reason for my name not being called for the auction. But there was no explanation for it even from the Master, other than his telling me, "Your place here, just do as you are told."

Having lost out to participate in the auction, now I find myself being the only one putting in a fourteen-hour workday. It is now my second week completed as trained when the word comes to me that I am to be interviewed for a job. To go out into the world outside! Make money to spend on clothes to suit me. Go to the movies that I had heard of but had seen only once through the generosity of the manager of a newly opened theatre. At school I had earned complimentary tickets for academic achievements but was forbidden to accept them. The thoughts of that prospective job interview made my days seem brighter and the work less arduous until the meeting with my near future boss.

It happened. The meeting was satisfactory to my employer but I would have to wait one month before starting. The date was set for Monday, February 15, 1915. A day that seemed to hold no significance at the time, but at least it gave me hope as the days passed.

During my waiting period, word was received that the assistant to the inmate who assisted the Master, had been arrested, tried and sentenced to pay a fine of one pound for the crime of leaving the institution with the clothes on his person. He had answered the call of a wealthy man who wanted volunteers to join a regiment that he had founded, financed and equipped, to take part in the relief of Antwerp. Six hundred were mustered who took part on the battle-front. Six weeks later they returned with sixty men, one who was the criminal.

Here were another six hundred who rode into the "Valley of Death," whose accomplishments were ridiculed and made to look like a farce, in this country that was constantly at war. Also consider this man who had committed such a dastardly crime. He was sixty-three years old at the time and one of his most treasured possessions was a table knife with a broken blade with which he shaved himself each day. There apparently was one problem with the knife. He could not keep the blade above his skin. Nevertheless, when he was with us he was the epitome of smartness in the uniform of a pauper. Perhaps he had the allusion that he was in command of a platoon of the line when he drilled us kids.

It was doubtful that the court collected the fine from him. He returned to the Union following the trial but did not get his rank returned as drill instructor of the miniature paupers' platoon-his punishment for getting his clothes soiled with the mud of "No Man's Land."

4

Apprenticed As Bellhop

After more than ten years, the day had arrived for me to go on the outside; into the world that I had been trained to face with hard work and obedience to everyone older than myself. As that person would be my elder, I would speak only when spoken to and yet I had not been advised as to what the consequences would be, were there any violations on my part of these rigid rules.

Regardless, I had to leave, not that I had any desire to stay. At the same time I was not elated over the fact that this was to be the termination of my incarceration in this Workhouse, the Union, or the Poorhouse: a trinity of three in one or one in three.

At the appointed hour I was sent to the main hall to meet the matron of the institution in order to be outfitted with two suits unlike anything the average boy wore. Also, three striped shirts that resembled mattress ticking, three Eton collars, a black tie, three pairs of socks, an overcoat, and a pair of shoes that were ordinarily worn by the girls, were presented to me. It was requested that I stand and watch this person stamp the usual brand on each item of apparel. As she stamped them I folded and placed them in a little trunk.

After a lecture lasting at least ten minutes with the final quote, "If your work on this job is not satisfactory you will be sent back and kept here until you are twenty-one." So, for the unpardonable crime of being an orphan and serving nearly eleven years of harsh treatment, that society feels is insufficient payment, another six years would be added to my sentence as being on probation. Another six years, making me fifteen now and I was wondering how they are calculating my age without knowing my birth statistics, or did they know?. With preparations completed, a dark grey-jacketed inmate-the emblem worn by them on orders, of course, telling the world that he was over sixty and a resident of the "Old-Mens'-Ward"-was summoned to carry my little trunk with the institution's loaned belongings to my place of forced employment, The Grand Hotel.

The hotel was located at the farthest end of the town from the Hotel of the Destitute. In order to get there we had to walk the entire length of Union Road, then to follow the tram-car tracks for a distance of a mile and a half. Not even a penny each was given to us for the carfare. As we walked along, I occasionally offered to carry the trunk but he refused and kept going without stopping until we reached our destination.

Although I had been in this town for so many years I had not seen it-The Grand Hotel. Then we came upon it. Passing the main entrance, also the delivery entrance, into the saloon bar entrance we went, which was on the far side of the building.

Upon entering here, we were greeted by a lovely young woman who immediately went to a pump handle at the bar to draw a pint of brew for my escort and a lemonade for me before meeting the manager. It became evident to me that my partner had had this detail on previous occasions, when boys before me had left to work here. With my trunk put in a corner of the bar I then proceeded to the manager's office for orders, where I was handed a uniform. He then told me that the pay would be a half-crown per week, with working hours from seven in the morning till nine in the evening, with two hours off during the day, seven days a week. The uniform was green with red piping, consisting of a tunic with brass buttons (fifty-one in all) and I was to answer to the name of "Page."

I lost no time in getting into uniform. Lo and behold, this day being Monday, the first one in years that a dish of cold boiled mutton, mushy rice and cold suet pudding were not here for me to stare at. Yet those around me were complaining because it was "Toad in the Hole." It was a change that I enjoyed. I left the table satisfactorily replete and at the same time being able to converse over a most unusual meal.

With eagerness, I went upstairs to report to the hall-porter who informed me as to the work routine. To my surprise there were no floors to be scrubbed, as most of the cleaning was done at night. The cleaning required of me was a little floor polishing and some brass to be polished on the front doors, then the buttons on my tunic, then spending the rest of the day opening and closing the door for people entering and leaving.

Coming to this place was a complete change, in that I was the only boy around and my elders were mostly ladies and gentlemen who did not desire to be officious in requesting my services to do small favours yet they were gracious enough to thank me. That gave me a feeling of wanting to hide.

The War here was making changes daily. At the end of the first week both the hall and night-porters joined up but it did not create any problem for the manager to get replacements. The only difference was the quality of personnel. The night man was replaced by my doing one of his jobs at the end of the day and by having another boy from the Union to share the remainder of his work early each day. My additional work at the end of the day was to carry a large wooden tray with a piece of chalk, to collect the guests' shoes that would be put outside the doors. I put the number of the room on the soles then take them downstairs to polish early the following morning.

Whereas upon starting to work at the hotel, the manager had told me that I was to answer to the name of "Page" but with my having such a brass-bound uniform, "Buttons" was the name used. Then by having to polish the guests' shoes another title was bestowed on me. "Boots." In the event that a guest wanted to show his appreciation or dissatisfaction concerning his footwear and the shine thereon, he would ask to see Boots but he was referred to Buttons. From then on I was called Buttons or Boots.

One morning a Lieutenant Commander of the Royal Naval Air Service was expressing extreme dissatisfaction for the lack of shine on his knee-high leather boots that were used to wade in salt-water for his boarding a seaplane. He handed them to me with the order that they had to be returned within a half hour, with a bright shine. A Major standing near, awaiting the outcome of this tirade, called and took the boots, handing them to the owner and told him to do them himself or get one of his men to do the impossible.

I was not the immediate successor to the Boots who joined up because a man over service age was hired and when he took the tray to collect the shoes he did not take chalk. Therefore he was subjected to some sharp criticism as he carried the tray from one to three floors for the guests to select their shoes. Following the completion of the deliveries, the poor fellow quit, telling the manager that the job took too many hours.

The hall-porter to be hired was also well along the road in years and would not take the job without his wife being hired as a chamber-maid and she was handicapped with a severe loss of hearing problem. One day I was sent to the floor on which she worked, with typed orders to get a room ready that had been reserved by telephone. Knowing that it would be virtually useless to go on the floor calling her name, I used my judgment in going to the rooms with open doors. One room that I entered with the door partially opened, lo and behold, I saw "September Morn" on a day in June. This lady had just taken a bath and that the bathroom being across the hall, she had returned to her room without closing the door. I barged in to look for and expecting to see the chambermaid, instead, I saw the beautiful wife of a young Naval lieutenant standing in front of the only full-length mirror that the hotel had, completely nude. I ran upstairs to give the note to another chamber-maid to deliver, without giving her a reason for my not doing so.

Later the lady came downstairs to leave and it being my duty to open the door for her, I did so with my head down staring at the floor, wondering what to say should she question me. Instead, she put me at ease by placing her hand under my chin, raising my head to look at her smile. The smile that came from me in return was twofold in its purpose. One was out of gratitude. The other was admiration for her beauty of both figure and features; with hair that was raven-black and sparkling eyes, beneath them, two rows of dazzling, even teeth. With a, "Thank you," for my opening the door, that was the sole extent of the conversation regarding that embarrassing incident.

Then later there were other incidents of invasion of privacy due to the maid's deafness and not by me. Thus it became necessary to discharge her and so went the hall-porter, too. The one who replaced him was a young man of eligible service age but with the handicap of having lost his right hand in France.

In the front of the Grand Hotel was a small park in the centre of which was a band-stand and this young fellow was in an Army band that used to give concerts on Sunday afternoons. This hall-porter's specialty was giving a cornet solo from the balcony outside of the room that I experienced my embarrassment. Of that incident no one ever knew, at least as far as I was concerned, because the feeling was shameful. However, in the course of a few months this man was the sixth hall-porter and his musical career was brought to an abrupt end. As there was no cross channel passenger service, therefore, no money was to be made. So he left shortly thereafter. He came here upon being discharged from the Army through a recommendation of his bandmaster who was a friend of the manager's.

At that time I had learned about an opening in a hotel one block away that paid a shilling a week more than I was getting. With business being a little better, my horizons were brighter when I was accepted. So with a good feeling within, I confronted the manager of the Grand Hotel to give notice of my leaving at the end of one week, giving him the reason-to better myself. He appeared to take the matter quite graciously, when with a pleasant, "Good morning, Page," he beckoned me into his office. That was two days later. He asked me how much money had I in my pocket and to place it on the table, which I did. Totaling three and four pence were put down. Included in that amount were wages of the remainder of two days' tips. But to make sure the pockets were emptied, he ordered me to turn them inside out, at the same time remarking that business was slow. Then came the crusher. When he told me to don the uniform cap bearing the letters,

"Grand Hotel" in gold above the peak and at the same time wearing the brass bound uniform, he then said that the Master of the Poorhouse wanted to speak to me.

Four months prior to this, I had taken this walk in the outlandish clothes of an institution and now in the outstanding ones of another. The town was full of soldiers and sailors. Some by way of joking, would salute me. Some would ask from what regiment was I and so on, for a great part of the distance. There was no one that I knew to whom I could ask for tram-fare to relieve me of this discomfort. To make matters worse was the thought of my having to return the same way.

Knowing the short-cuts brought me some comfort because the meadows would not be populated but I wondered if the horses that would be grazing would charge or to bolt upon seeing a crowd of buttons coming towards them. However, they were not hostile in the least but as I walked there more hostility built inside of me towards the boss, the Headmaster and the whole human race.

Upon my arrival I was confronted with the "Authority" in the form of a plump, squat woman. The same one who upon leaving this building a matter of four months before, had outfitted me with the marked clothes. If in the event I left my sinecure, she would have me believe it was cause for me to be subjected for arrest like the elderly Army volunteer. There she was. Her head and breasts of equal size, resembling an inverted pawnbroker's sign, out to welcome me. With an admonishing finger to threaten me with the warning that I was to stay at the Grand Hotel or else be brought back to the inside of these walls until I reached the age of twenty-one.

After being lectured for five minutes and without being made to promise that the order would be obeyed, I then was permitted to leave for a return. Through the streets filled with uniforms, I received a reception similar to the one experienced a short time before. This time I felt dejected at the thought of being on parole for four to six years, depending upon what age I am given. I trudged the pavement to return to more incarceration. There was consolation in the thought that there was only a door being opened forever between freedom and me. When the opportunity arrives and by nurturing this thought, made my feet feel lighter and filled me with hope. This hope enabled me to ignore the remarks of Tommies as they passed.

I rationalized that the reason for the length of parole being indefinite was due to the fact that I had never been informed as to my date or place of birth. Then as I pondered over this, it dawned upon me that nobody cared and precautions were taken that I would never know. Therefore, I had gone this far without a birthday.

As I was in the vicinity of the school I had attended, it occurred to me to visit and enquire of my Schoolmaster, about the information that he might have regarding these matters. But I was forgetting at the same time that the uniform on me was most inappropriate.

However, he greeted me. Then hearing of my mission he went to the register to refer to the record that was there, when I began schooling there. He stated that June tenth was my day of birth (no year recorded) and day of enrollment was June 10, 1907 but beyond this there was no further entry about me. Blank! No year of birth was recorded? I did not have to think hard for why no year was given yet is used as my date of school enrollment. So even this scanty data was questionable. The past was hazy yet I recalled the utility pantry. I've scrubbed its floor too often not to remember being slapped down to it so long ago. My left eye also remembers.

The Schoolmaster was curious to know why I had come that distance in the regalia on me. To his way of thinking, he stated that he would have remembered me without it. Then he requested me to sit while I related the conditions that existed in the Poorhouse for the kids whom this man liked for the way they behaved. Before I left he gave me some encouragement by reminding me that I was now on the outside. He showed considerable concern and told me this was the first interview that he had ever held regarding the care or lack of it for the Union boys. During our talk he mentioned that the Army would be occupying the section of the Union that the children had and they were to be transported to a town some six miles away. He added that he would be sorry to lose them especially because of their regular attendance.

The conversation at one point turned to those of us from the Mansion who had left and were in the military services. Quite a number of them had visited me because down through the years the Grand Hotel used young paupers for its' services. So when these servicemen came back it was out of curiosity as to who would be at the front door. I rattled off the names of those I had seen, whereupon he took pencil and paper with the intent to have a separate Roll of Honour and amongst them were two who would never return.

Both boys had left the Union three years before me. One was found a job working in the scullery of a boardinghouse, with room and board, but the pay would not be much. The other boy was apprenticed to the barber who had the contract for the inmates of the Union, for a wage of one whole penny per week with room and board. It was doubtful that lather boys ever got tips so with his apprenticeship incomplete his life was taken along with the other lad's. Both of them were each in the Union seven years to my knowledge. The Schoolmaster remembered them well because he had them for pupils for so long.

They volunteered their services but it was doubtful that it was for patriotic reasons as much as for avarice, because being in service the barber-apprentice would get forty-two times as much in pay each week and the training would cause him no hardship. He also would be clothed, sheltered and fed.

It was lunchtime recess at school therefore, I had to leave him with the promise that this would not be my last visit with him. The walk back through the main streets of the town filled me with dread and disgust. What does the future have for me in these conditions?

Army barracks surrounded the town that was in a valley, through which the main street ran. A day didn't pass that there was not a regiment of soldiers spearheaded by a band to lead them to the transport. Its destination was "No Man's Land."

On this day when I left the school, strains of martial music could be heard and on reaching the main street I stood waiting for their passing. Amongst them was a Union boy. My polished brass-buttons had caught his eye. He waved for me to notice him and as luck would have it, he was on the end of the four-deep columns, so I was able to keep stride with him on the sidewalk for the last mile that I had to go. My emotions got the better of me as I said, "Good-bye," to one of hundreds whom I had seen come and go through the portals of poverty. He was to go where? "The Valley of Death, etc." Why?

He had a younger brother whose whereabouts were unknown since he left us. He left this older brother who also became the possession of the Dover Union and now who was being sent to an unknown place. Brothers separated by circumstance. The mutual feelings that we had for each other were the result of being together with so many of us Pauper boys. There existed among us a relationship due in a large part to the contempt that the people had for us when we were segregated. Now that the country was in conflict with others, the property of the local taxpayers in boys, without any question, was integrated.

At the Grand Hotel the manager was waiting for me with a barrage of questions, as to the reason for my taking as much time to return but I refused to answer them. The thought came to me that he needed me more than I needed him. In the first place the Union boys would not be available. Also, there was plenty of work for boys to replace the men who had joined up but for all reasons there was no sense in giving back-talk. Although it was late he told me to go to lunch. Actually, it was time for my two hours recess and when I brought this to his attention he stated that he thought I had a nerve requesting the time off.

It was a rule of the house that an employee could have a beverage from the bar only with his lunch. I went for my soda and was questioned by the lovely dispenser of liquors, about my being so late. So instead of taking the drink to the lunch, I brought it to the bar and spent the two hours relating first my assignment for that day, then telling of the previous eleven years and now to have to serve parole here for at least another four years or more. Although she had been in this place a few years and had seen Union boys come and go as page-boys, yet she had never questioned them. She now remarked that she found them well-behaved. Having gained her confidence, she said that she would make arrangements for me to run away and go to sea.

Every evening the hotel bar was filled with Naval Officers from the numerous vessels moored to buoys in the harbour but they could do nothing for me because they were not in command. However, I was advised to be patient. The reason for the bar being filled with Naval Officers only was that Army Officers were not allowed to drink in public bars. To get around that order, the billiard-room adjoined the bar and was frequented by them, whereby the drinks were served to them through a small window in the far corner that was situated behind the bar.

Around the same time each evening the Major Provost Marshall would make his rounds of the hotels to see that the law was being observed. Walking fast through the place he would first start opening the billiard-room door to look all around from that point. Next, always seeing young gentlemen with commissions seemingly intent on playing billiards with many of their kind as interested spectators, he would leave to enter the bar where there was never enough room for him, with it being filled with Naval Officers and the manager socializing for free drinks. For a special reason the Provost never caught any violator and that reason was myself.

Knowing the approximate time of his coming, I would take a position where he could not see me. Then upon his entrance I would run to open the door and call out, "Provost," and run out of the side exit, next through the front door and take up my position to open the door for his departure. At the call of Provost, the barmaid would gather the glasses and close the window that had a cover to conceal it.

When all was back to normal a big second lieutenant would take me to the billiard-room where I had to have a whiskey with soda and a penny or two from each one as a reward. At the first attempt at refusing to imbibe, my arms were held and my nose was pinched until my mouth was compelled to open. Alas, this was enough to convince me that it would be advisable to drink of my own free will. That one drink each night was enough to make me look stupid at every one for whom the door was opened.

When the manager first saw me in this condition he questioned me as to how I got loaded and asked where it came from and who served me. The information that he sought was not forthcoming from me and the barmaid could not account for it. Even the Army Officers put on an act of ignorance when asked. That alone was enough to tell them that I had not squealed. This continued each night, with my drink followed by the Manager's interrogation, until one night he was doing his act with me when a Lieutenant Commander was about to leave. This gentleman was noted for being a good drinker in this place when on shore leave. Whole evenings he would spend drinking and he was known to carry it well. But as the Manager was reprimanding me for my stupor, this officer turned to him, asking for his reason for not being joined up instead of sponging drinks and with that he sent a fist to the jaw and flattened him.

Following the encounter he came towards the door, which I opened for him. I then ran down the four steps to open the outer door. Here he hesitated until the door behind us closed. While approaching me, he was saying that he was being transferred but that he would pass the word on to his replacement to help me run away to go to sea. He told me that "Bubbles," the barmaid, told him all about me and the probation time I was serving. At the same time he was speaking he was expressing his contempt for the person he left in a horizontal position with an equal strain on all parts.

From this moment on a complete change in attitude came over me toward the world. Now I had the thought that after so long a period of time there were at least two elders had respect and compassion for me and they were to be instrumental in improving my conditions. The first steps had been taken for my leaving to go to sea. In what type or purpose of vessel had never entered my head. It was something to which I could look forward. Then up those steps, seemingly in one bound, I took my position at the door again. There in the lounge the Manager was being revived while seated on a large chair by three young Army Officers who had placed him there. One of them left to question me as to what had happened to lead to this fracas. He, being one of my drinking partners, I confided in him only to learn he had no more pity for the Manager than the one who had delivered the knock-out punch. He too, asked for the reason for his not being joined up. He had been rated as unfit because of a speech impediment that was only slight. Other than this imperfection, he was six feet tall, not overweight in the least and the only one to spend entire evenings in the bar in mufti. The Army

Officers never saw this side of the Manager's behavior due to the restrictions placed on them. In fact, they had no occasion to meet.

After this event, each following evening, I looked at every Naval Officer whom I thought would be the one to help shanghai me. As he would enter I would search for a sign that he was acquainted with the predicament of my lot.

A full month passed. Then one evening after closing-time for the bar, a tall, slender, white-haired Lieutenant Commander began placing a monocle to his eye. He addressed me by saying, "Are you the young man who wants to go to sea?" That question brought the Manager to a halt as he had been following this gentleman.

I replied, "Yes, sir." He then told me to be on the Naval Pier at nine-thirty the following morning, from where the small boat would take us to the ship to leave to go on patrol.

With that he bade me, "Good-night."

With the Manager knowing this, there was only one course of action for me to take. When I got off duty I hurriedly changed into a blue suit, put the bed-pillow under the blankets and without a word to anyone took the longer way around the hotel, in order to avoid passing the front door and I made for the Naval Pier approximately twelve hours ahead of schedule. The pier was not open to the public. Its name had been changed from Promenade Pier and was now being used as a signal station for the ships moored to buoys in the harbour.

Therefore, at the shore end was stationed a special policeman. He had been informed of my coming by the white-haired Lieutenant Commander but not at this hour and he was to pass the word along to the one who would be on duty in the morning. After a short introduction and an explanation, combined with a request for permission to stay in his small hut with him, he consented but I had to give a full story of the facts leading to this predicament. He had been born and raised in this town of Dover yet he could hardly believe that children from the Union went into the world lacking guidance and workable skills. Some sleep overcame me while seated on a stool with my back against the side of the hut and I awakened on a new dawn, waiting for that appointed hour.

It came and the Lieutenant Commander escorted me to the small boat, telling the crew that I was a new member of the ship's complement. It was a short distance from the pier to the ship and as soon as we got aboard the boat was hoisted. The Lieutenant Commander took me below and introduced me to the Steward, having assigned me to being his assistant. Then leaving us he went on the bridge.

5

Frenchy Goes To Sea

The time is 0945 or nine forty-five in the morning on March 16, 1916. Today is Friday and presumed to be an unlucky day to go to sea.

There is no wind therefore the sea is calm. As the ship proceeds slowly toward the entrance to Dover Harbour, all deckhands keep a sharp look-out for the concrete breakwater from which comes the blasts of its fog-horn. The fog is very dense as we clear the Harbour.

In doing so (just barely) a vessel is sighted quite close to us when it strikes a mine. As soon as it happens a seaman on our ship, referring to me, says, "This kid is a Jonah."

Another man attempts to correct him by saying, "We did not strike it so why blame the kid?"

The ship is a minesweeping steam trawler that is to be commissioned. She is the H.M.S. Kings Grey and does not need assistance although she is taking in water in the forward part. There are no casualties. Grey's skipper calls through the megaphone that he would beach her.

I am now a crewmember of H.M.S. James Fletcher: a vessel armed with two six-pounder guns. She is to serve as flagship to a fleet of herring fishing vessels, commissioned and armed by Dover with one three-pounder gun and we are part of the Dover Patrol. (Our other gun is on some other vessel).

After proceeding slowly for two hours, following the first incident of the effects of war, something looms ahead what appears to be a rock formation. As the ship gets closer it turns out to be many bales of cork, boxes of tomatoes, barrels of rum and large cases of smoked meat. A dozen bales of cork are hauled aboard when the barrels of rum are sighted, so in order to make room for them, back goes most of the cork. In its stead comes sixteen barrels with hog heads full of rum tallying to two cases of liquor. Each barrel contains half of a large hog already butchered and smoked. We gather many boxes of fresh tomatoes that are individually wrapped in tissue paper and nicely packed in sawdust.

There is no evidence of a ship having sunk. The only conclusion drawn from this bounty is that the vessel sunk sometime before. The hatches must have burst causing this cargo to surface. This conclusion is drawn from the fact that fresh tomatoes would not be loaded on a ship to be plying the waters for even a few days. Yet when we get them they are perfectly ripe. So to prevent spoiling, the Commander distributes them amongst the ships that hove in sight. In which case they would be within hailing distance to us because of the dense fog.

While this is going on I have been put to work making three officers' bunks, cleaning their cabins and getting the Wardroom ready for lunch. Then the Steward, who seems pleased with what has been done, calls to me, "Hear me now, get your self some time out an' get on deck for airin'."

Once there, a crewman, the leading seaman gunner, spots me and orders me to follow him below to the cabin that has four bunks. He goes to his bunk, reaches in and produces a one-pound can of tobacco with cigarette papers. He demonstrates the art of rolling cigarettes and orders me to learn how to roll them until twenty are made. He comes back a little later with the order that at nine-thirty every day that would be a part of my work. My training from the Union is still a part of me; to be obedient and respectful to my elders. The thought never occurs to me to question authority. I am thinking that everyone else has it but me. The first day goes by smoothly until it is time to turn in, whereupon I ask the Steward, "Where am I to sleep?"

Then it comes to him with a chuckle, "Why, this is sweet! Your only empty berth is the stateroom, my lucky lad."

This vacant stateroom is similar to the Commander's accommodation but is reserved for any high-ranking officer such as the Captain of the Drifter Patrol, in case he decides to make a trip. "No Sir, Steward, I will not go there," I stoutly reply, thinking he is jesting.

The matter is brought to the attention of the Commander in the presence of a Lieutenant who had been the Skipper of this ship before the war. Without hesitation the best and only berth is given to me and at the same time the Commander adds that when the war is over he would take me to Australia to live with him on a large sheep ranch, if I am in accord.

I am so filled with accord that I can hardly sputter, "Oh yes, Sir!"

Being informed that it is not advisable to close a cabin door shut while at sea, I close it as far as the hook would permit, then kneel beside the bunk and say a prayer of thanks for what this most wonderful day in my life has brought; especially for the bright future. With the door partially open, I am privy to hearing the more conversation.

The Commander continues to converse with the Lieutenant, telling him that he has no son or daughter to whom he could will his wealth. Having been briefed as to my background he states that I would fit into his void. The thought of this good fortune along with the sound of the ship's whistle constantly blowing due to the fog, keeps me from sleeping for a long while. The bell on the bridge also keeps adding one sound to each half-hour that passes to tell us the time.

This then, is the end of the first day of freedom. But then again how free am I? Since stepping aboard this vessel and taking into consideration the dense fog with its lurking dangers and the mines that are not visible in clear weather, how free am I? That one mine had already taken its toll and what of the unintentional jettisoned cargo that may have taken lives with it? Yet before sleep comes to overtake me, all I could see is a bright future that is to come to me after this war would end.

The Steward could see that I am well experienced at making the officers' bunks, cleaning their cabins, the Ward-room and polishing the brass. This gives him more time to devote to his catering, resulting in his showing every consideration to make conditions pleasant for me. The one thing that he has to tell me to do often is to go on deck occasionally to get the air because my prior training had been to be confined to the one area where my duties were. Other than these reminders, he is appreciative.

Going on deck means meeting the crew, not collectively though. Taking a peek at the stokehold, then the engine-room and the operators, I become aware that anyone of them is old enough to be my grandfather. The concept of war is gradually seeping into me.

What a difference there is between land and sea, I so think. The glaring posters ashore are bearing the slogan, "If you are a young man between the ages of eighteen and thirty-five, Your King and Country Need You." That billboard is not visible to the ships at sea with crews such as man this vessel. Nearly fifty percent of these men are well over the military age, but who would know the ship better than its original personnel?

This ship is now a "man-of-war" with its peacetime crew added to it; a white haired Commander, two Petty Officers that are on pension, two Signal Boys, some Naval Reserve seamen and one Naval Reserve Officer. Actually there is not one Royal Navy man aboard. Regardless, they are all very friendly and unaffected by the rank and commission bestowed upon them.

At the appointed time the scheduled cigarettes are made in much less time than it took on the first day. But because that is the number consumed daily by this man, he would not permit me to make more.

The second and third days pass without incidence although the fog remains just as dense. Then the day following these is the end of the trip on patrol. On the fifth day the fog finally lifts. From this time on because of routine, it would be three days out then three in. We are moored to a buoy at the end of a row occupied by a flotilla of destroyers that are all named after different tribes of the world. As no two tribes seem to be alike, that may have accounted for their being named the "Tribal Class." Originally there were ten that constituted the sixth flotilla but two were already out of commission. Knocked out of service, they were the H.M.S. Maori and the H.M.S. Viking. The latter one had six funnels. The names of some of the others in service are the H.M.S. Zulu, Cossack, Crusader, Nubian, Tartar and Amazon.

In fact, the Dover Harbour is full of vessels that by far are not the most modern. Being basically a fish producing country, England's aquae-craft amounted to any floating structures. With the exception of the monitors being built for the sole purpose of the bombardment of the Belgian Coast, the others are makeovers. Added to the monitors are two four-funneled light cruisers, a few submarines with a parent ship and an obsolete battleship. This is the extent of the Royal Navy based in the nearest port to the Continent where all the action is taking place.

Separated from these ships of the line are the steam trawlers, minesweepers, paddle-steamers and side-wheels that comprise the drifters and yacht patrols. The H.M.S. James Fletcher is one of four of the yacht patrol and this is the Dover Patrol in its entirety.

The schedule is the rotation of three days on patrol and three days in port. At the end of three months without further patrol, the ship is docked for overhaul. At this time the crew gets seven days leave. But because I have no home the Steward is given my leave, unknown to the Commander. It is during this first week of leave that pay is due but the officer whose duty it generally is has gone on leave, so another one takes care of the matter. However, after paying the hands still left aboard, he comes on deck and upon seeing me, says, "Kid, I have no pay for you."

"I reply, "Sir, I don't get any."

He then asks me if I have been signed on.

I answer, "No, Sir."

He then asks, "What do you do for money when you go ashore?"

I reply, "I do not go ashore."

"Why?" he asks.

I answer, "Because I have no uniform, therefore I would be detained for questioning."

"How long have you been aboard?"

"Three months, Sir."

"That means that you have missed pay six times. Also, if something happened to you in that time, if, as you say, you have no home or any relatives, then your disappearance would not be known to anyone?"

With a shrug of my shoulders, I reply, "Yes, Sir."

He promises that he would get matters corrected as soon as his relief comes back from leave. This officer, before joining up, had been a mate on a freighter and now has the rank of a Lieutenant in the Royal Naval Reserve. He is a handsome man about five feet ten, in his mid-twenties, with white even teeth and jet-black hair. He speaks with a fairly broad cockney accent and never makes any attempt to hide it.

A few days later his relief comes aboard and though he is anxious to leave, this Lieutenant takes time out to give this man a calling-down in my behalf, with a flow of expletives befitting a man from the East-end of London. The excuse was that he (the pay officer) did not know my situation.

My champion soon reminds him of his complaining about the kid having the nicest cabin and also asks him, "What right have you to give the boy's leave to the steward?"

He replies, "The boy has no home."

"That being so," comes the reply, "don't you think that the kid would like to see the sights of London?" With that retort, he leaves to catch his train.

While this verbal exchange is going on I hide in the fidley (a narrow platform near the top of the boiler). When I meet this Officer later, having to prepare and serve his lunch, he does not utter one word in connection with this affair. The meal passes with his being in a sullen mood. It is evident that what he had been told has taken effect.

The week went by with his having little to say to me although we are the only occupants of the Wardroom. (The Commander had an apartment ashore that he shared with his wife whom he had brought with him from Australia. He left his ranch in the care of a manager).

Unknown to anyone of the few who are still aboard, this Lieutenant went to the Admiral's office to report that the Commander, when at sea, would come on the bridge intoxicated. Apparently, there was a hearing of some kind, still unknown to us.

The Commander comes aboard to tell me that he has invited some officers from the battleship to have lunch to celebrate his fifty-sixth birthday. The catering is to be done by the Grand Hotel, with one of the waiters to serve the luncheon on board. A delicious meal is served but only one guest comes. However, this gentleman (my Commander) did not seem to be the least upset as he relates to this much younger officer his experiences of his thirty years of duty, beginning with the Naval College. After lunch the Commander went to his cabin for a minute or two, then both went ashore. Meanwhile the Lieutenant kept out of the way, precisely, hiding.

It is not until all hands are back from their leave that the news breaks about the Commander having handed in his resignation rather than face a court-martial and he never returns aboard. At the time he is celebrating his birthday he is actually celebrating his leaving.

When the cockney Lieutenant hears about it he goes straight to the new Commander with remarks to the effect that he had gone to that trouble just to get the kid out of the state cabin. It is the first thing I have to do-to leave the state cabin. But there is not a single berth elsewhere, not until a signal-boy tells me that he has a hammock which could be slung underneath a skylight aft.

Once again I am the exception, being the only one aboard to sleep in a hammock. Without a doubt such a bed is very comfortable providing it is slung in an appropriate location. Whereas it is the rule that this form of sleeping accommodation is to be lashed and stowed when not in use but there is no place for it, so there it has to stay to catch the water that splashes in with bad weather. The head portion is over the foot of two bunks. The other end is over the coal-burning heater but at a safe height from the risk of its catching fire. Yet at the same time it is in a cloud of three cigarette smokers and one most obnoxious pipe that may or may not have been the cause of my severe "mal-de-mer" but it is most certainly not a cure.

Personally, the pipe-smoker is not obnoxious. He is a very nice fellow with an outstanding talent for accuracy. He would lie in his bunk, in a horizontal position with an equal strain on all of his parts, eyes closed with pipe in mouth, puffing on same until he had the desire to spit and that takes place very frequently-after about every three puffs. Without batting an eyelash, he would raise the pipe in his hand and with accuracy aim his expectoration that would sizzle on the stove-top thus clearing the underneath of the hammock by a foot. It is in the month of June when I first come to my new berth so there is no fire in the stove. But there is a wet spot on the stove at this time.

The morning following our leaving the dock to get to the mooring buoy, the Lieutenant decides to have me sign on at the Customhouse and give me to understand that he would do the talking for me. Now I learn why he will talk for me. When I first went aboard this ship and was asked my name by the Steward. I hesitated then, giving the Lieutenant the impression that I was stupid not to know my name. This question had taken me by surprise. I had immediately realized that "Frenchy" is not an appropriate name to be used in the British Navy so I again settle for Freddie, from my school days.

As soon as the Lieutenant mentions this name to the Customs Officer, I feel compelled to interrupt, to add a pretty typical English surname that the Headmaster once accused me of possibly owning. Errington. I had informed my companion, the Lieutenant, of this just before entering the Customhouse. But the Lieutenant, who had been a fisherman before signing into the Navy and now has a commission, adds an, "aitch" to the front of it. Now I am Fred Herrington. It is a common trait with him. As an example, while at sea the Commander would call to him to ask if he was there. The reply would always be, "Hi Ham, Sir." With this person it is a clear case of putting a beggar on horseback. Nevertheless, I feel no more like a Freddie Herrington or Errington as I did being Froggie or Frenchy. Following my name being entered into the records, the next question is, "Where were you born?"

This time the Lieutenant comes to my rescue right away by saying, "Dover." Then calling me to one side he asks if I remember the day when I first came aboard.

"It was on St. Patrick's Day, Sir."

So he gives the date as March ninth. Whether he knows differently I do not know but as I am not being deprived I am overtaken by a little bit of larceny and remain silent. That short ceremony terminates three months of service in the Royal Navy without my having been enlisted and also being enlisted for eight days that were not served.

By way of appeasing me, the Lieutenant, for not having given me leave earlier, now gives me the rest of the day off, along with a pass to enable me to return. As I am not in uniform, also without a penny, I could not go far. At the mention of the last item he hands me a half-crown as a loan and he would take it from my pay. With this vast sum, it is expected of me to eat and find entertainment for the next nine hours. Therefore, the only alternative would be to walk the streets. While doing this the news is being sent out that the Empire's leading General had been lost at sea on his way to Russia. Shortly after hearing this, I am walking along a side street and see a young soldier crying aloud as though heart-broken.

The first thought that comes to me is, could it be that he thinks so much of this General? The same one (General) to whom he (this bereaved young soldier) had answered his call? That so many more men had done nearly two years before? But in a matter of a few seconds later that theory is dispelled.

A motherly type of woman goes to console him and asks him what the trouble is. Between loud sobs he blurts out to her that he had been to France and had been wounded five times. "and now I am being sent over again, this very night," he is shuttering while crying.

He, like millions of other citizens, had volunteered to "do his bit." The meaning of the word in itself implies that it is a small particle of the whole yet does not clearly define the exact amount. Nevertheless, because he has two feet to walk on, two hands with which to carry a rifle and with forced intent to kill or maim complete strangers, he is expected to obey the command. While under the influence of alcohol do men give false courage of themselves, I wonder? Five times wounded. However, had he sufficient training in real combat to fire a bullet or to stop one again? The question is always the same in situations of this nature, "Whom does one kill and for what?" Sorting priorities was not coming easy for me.

Shortly after witnessing this sad sickening scene the Military Police march him back to his barracks. Coincidental as it seems to be, it might raise the question, "Does a soldier cry over the loss of a General?" Certainly not one who has been in the "Valley of Death," so glorified, instead of being horrified by Lord Alfie.

My one day of leave is spent in a more lonely manner than if I had returned to the Union and being the only one in it. There is not a soul whose home I could visit, so the day is spent walking the side streets to mostly avoid the numerous officers of the four branches of the British Service. By my being aboard ship there is a measure of companionship with men from different parts of the country.

There is one seaman in particular who is from the Isle of Man and who since returning from leave has nothing on his mind but Mary Ann. He carries on so much about her. But she is not his wife as he has never been married. Although he is fifty or more years old he does not get involved with anyone else of the fairer sex. His job aboard ship is assistant cook. As such, he does not keep watch therefore, he could shout this woman's name to the annoyance of both the watches when they are below. This behaviour goes on for two weeks while every moment he is awake. Fortunately nobody considers harming him for want of lost sleep. Up until the time that this shouting obsession overcomes him, he has always been a very congenial shipmate. He takes good care that the new Commander gets his share of harassment to gain his point. After two weeks without any letup he is sent to the sickbay, ashore.

This is the second man from the ship to my knowledge to be sent to the hospital since my joining her. The first one had been put ashore for that reason a month earlier and the news of his passing away at the age of twenty-eight from tuberculosis reaches us just at this time. He was the one who referred to me as a "Jonah." During the two months that I was his shipmate he was always friendly, even to me. The crew missed him very much. Some of them had known him all his life. Later it was the consensus that had he been given a proper physical examination at the time of his being commandeered, his end may not have come so soon to one so young. He had been a constant pipe-smoker and being confined in close overcrowded quarters certainly did not help his unknown condition. For that matter, with my having officially become a member of His Majesty's Armed Forces, I also was enlisted without being checked health-wise.

The new Commander is a Reserve Lieutenant with no more rank than the one who had been the skipper in peacetime. That sets this Skipper talking again as to the reason for his not getting the command. What he does not know is the fact that the new man in charge had received training in gunnery while doing reserve drill before the war. There are many merchant and passenger ships prior to his responsibilities that are manned by crews who have been in the reserve.

With the new command comes a new schedule that instead of going on patrol for three days and with three in shore, it changes to four out and two in. One advantage of this is getting to know the crew. One amongst them is a white-haired stoker of about sixty who would never go below deck while at sea, only to do his firing and then he would take every opportunity available to return deck-side. At mealtime he would bring his plate to eat in the fidley, also that is where he would sleep. He would wear little clothing that hangs loosely, shoes that are never laced, all ready for quick stripping in case of emergency, clearly depicting that he is really scared.

The reason for his being scared is that he is one of two survivors from a ship of the Yacht Patrol. In reality, he is the only survivor, strange as it may seem. His ship had left Dunkirk as an escort to a new monitor that was to shell the fortifications on the coast of Belgium, an operation that had not been done for months, pending the arrival of these new monitors with shallow draft and twelve-inch turret guns. The head (commander) of this splash (action) was of the opinion that he could resume where he had stopped some months previously.

As soon as the two ships got to about five miles off shore the guns there opened up, hitting the monitor repeatedly and the Yacht amidships, killing all on board except the stoker who is now with us. As his ship was sinking, his leg got jammed between the stays and bulwarks caused by the explosion, but at the last moment he was freed as the vessel takes the final plunge to "Davy Jones's locker." After being rescued he was transferred to the H.M.S. James Fletcher and given a certain amount of money for clothing allowance. He is back on the job without a physical examination and to all appearances he is not injured. He also is about sixty years old. In order to make room for him another stoker gets promoted to the engineering section. The survivor's condition was brought to the attention of the new Commander who lost no time in getting this man his discharge.

The other survivor of this sunken ship was the signal-boy who at the last moment was ordered ashore to take something to the Commodore, then to wait on the quay for his ship to return. He waited for a ship that never did return. He was transferred to another ship in the Yacht Patrol. That ship was sunk later, after having struck a mine and he was saved in a similar manner as the previous one. On the day of leaving Dover he was detailed once again to deliver something to the office of the Captain of the Drifter Patrol and he was to be on the Naval pier three days later but "O She Never Returned."

One Lieutenant who was saved was brought into the Grand Hotel while I was employed there, still in his wet uniform and shivering. He was taken to the bar for first-aid. Both Army and Navy Officers threw their overcoats over him as he took medicine made in Scotland, while a hot bath was being drawn for him. He was carried upstairs and put into the bath-tub with just his head above water, in order for him to take more from the bottle. While these proceedings were going on a collection was made for his being able to stay for a week. At the same time I was detailed to take his clothes to the boiler-room to dry and to tell the chamber-maid to put three hot-water bottles into his bed. When she had done that, unknown to anyone, she waited in the room, undoubtedly for the purpose of expecting a tip. However, when the rescued Lieutenant was lifted out of the tub and dried off by this sophisticated team of medics, at the same time being unable to stand due to the booze that had been pumped into him, he was rushed along the hall into his room while I kept look-out. A loud scream went up as he entered the room.

Then one of the group said, "You may have seen a drunken sailor, dear, but have you never seen one naked?"

Needless to say she did not wait for a tip but she had caused other guests to leave their rooms when hearing what had caused her screaming. They mostly enjoyed the joke. That all happened on a Sunday evening so that there was no way that the Lieutenant could buy pajamas and this man (if seen walking in the hall to reach certain facilities, wrapped in a sheet) could easily frighten somebody. One of the guests who had joined the party loaned him a suit but by this time the man had passed out. Now it was up to those who had stripped him to clothe him. I was kept busy running to the bar for glasses, bottles and food from the kitchen.

The signal-boy who had survived the second sinking was transferred to the H.M.S. James Fletcher and the feeling among the crew was that they all felt safe while he was aboard, following the legend that had been attached to him. At the same time that the war broke out he was serving an apprenticeship on a merchant ship that was commandeered. Instead of being allowed to remain on her he was sent to the Naval Barracks to learn signaling. This was something in which he excelled and enjoyed practicing with a signalman at the station on the Naval Pier. This team was acknowledged to be the best in this port. Besides doing that he studied navigation for the time when with enough sea-time, he could pass a Board of Trade examination to obtain a Mate's license.

Another incident in which this signal-boy was involved was on the night of January 9, 1916, when the H.M.S. James Fletcher rammed a submarine. This happened about two months prior to my joining her and this is the way this event was discussed. After the crew had been ashore to collect prize money in the amount of one thousand pounds, to be given for the sinking of an enemy submarine by a British ship although its crew were not full-time servicemen in the Royal Navy.

The collision occurred without either vessel having seen one another. The H.M.S. James Fletcher at the time was patrolling at slow speed when she struck an object that was submerged and loud voices were heard coming from it. At the time of impact the signal-boy was said to be the only one with presence of mind to go to his station in action. He manned the searchlight, standing on the deck with bare feet and got quite a shock because the platform was damp with dew.

The money was allotted in this manner; the Officers were given ninety-seven pounds each, Petty Officers fifty-five, lower deck ratings thirty-two, signal-boy six. This prize money was not donated by the Admiralty or any department of the government but by a wealthy person, not known to the recipients.

The one deck-hand who stood up for me when I was called a "Jonah," was now undertaking to do something in the sense of fair play for the signal-boy. He gathered the crew around him and telling them that the Bunting Tosser (signal-boy) is entitled to, if not, more than what each man had received and he quoted a figure that each should donate to bring his share to parity. All complied readily except the Lieutenant who brought about the resignation of my prospective foster father. He was the only one to hold out. All the pleading and begging that the deckhand could muster did not shake one penny from the other man. Though an Officer and a supposed leader at the time of the collision, panic-stricken, he ran aft-calling for the men to lower the life-boat.

This deckhand standing five feet four inches, weighing one hundred pounds, is shaming another who is standing nearly six feet and weighing about two hundred thirty pounds. Still, he would not come across and I am there to witness the humiliation of a superior. The deckhand has to be admired for his straight forwardness without regard to rank and could be compared with the most accurate gun. However, the signal-boy gets an equal share and then the subject is brought up as to who should get the Distinguished Service Medal that will be sent from the War Department. After a group consultation, led by this champion of corrections, it is decided that the hardware be awarded to the Chief Petty Officer.

The Chief Petty Officer has white hair, is fifty-six years of age, enlisted as a boy and altogether served forty-three years in service. He has authority over the lower-hand ratings but never exercised it, except in one way that became completely unavoidable. That was in having been ordered to submit the list of defaulters: such as the men who miss the boat the night before without requesting all-night leave, as they would be coming aboard in the same boat as the Commander. Generally speaking, no one ever created any real problem for the Chief.

After picking up the sixteen barrels of rum on the first day, it is decided that one barrel at least, should be put below for home consumption. This suits the Chief just dandy, as he is accustomed to having a daily tot of the stuff for so many years. But because liquor is not being issued to auxiliary ships, he has been without his grog for some time. Therefore, every so often he would put a teapot inside a burlap bag and go below to fill it. Then coming on deck carrying a good load and shaking the bag he would stumble along the deck. Spilling the fluid, he would say, "Freddie, I've got a bird."

By his saying this, he means for me to be his decoy because the un-heroic Lieutenant is keeping watch on the barrel. He is annoyed at the Chief's constant trips to the barrel but is at a loss as to what action he should take. The Champion comes to aid him in his quandary by letting him know that the Chief could only take so much of this Jamaica rum then would have to quit and also, the Chief is the only one aboard ship interested in drinking the stuff. This advice is noticeably falling on deaf ears so to make his point he tells the Lieutenant that should he decide to report the Chief, that he, in turn, would report him for his lack of leadership, with many witnesses to support his charge. The advice terminates the "watch on the barrels."

6

The Dover Patrol

The Dover Patrol at this stage of the war is now a combination of three patrols: Drifter, Yacht and Barrage Patrols. The Barrage Patrol route consists of large buoys spaced about two-hundred fifty yards apart, running across the Straits from the Goodwin Sands, to a distance of three miles from the coast of France. Suspended between the buoys are steel nets at a depth of ten feet and beneath them are mines anchored to the bed of the sea. Such is the Barrage Patrol-to prevent enemy submarines from coming through the barriers. Also for additional security, sixty or more Drifters peruse the waterways to see that if a sub does manage to get through, they are to report same to one of the two Yachts that act as Flagship for them. These two Yachts are the only vessels with wireless telegraphy other than the Batteries on the breakwater of the Dover Harbour. On shore, the heaviest pieces of armament are the four six-pounders that belong on the two Yachts.

To prove the point to beware of sneak attacks, here is one example. On the night of October twenty-sixth, enemy destroyers get to within hailing distance of Dover Harbour, fire a few shells into the town as a calling-card and as a challenge to the Sixth Flotilla. They met the enemy or maybe it is the other way around, because no sooner does the H.M.S. Nubian clear the Dover Harbour entrance than she is torpedoed, resulting in her bows being blown off to the bridge. What is left of her is beached close to where the S.V. Prussean ran aground in 1913, just before the war. The Prussean is an all steel, full-rigged sailing-vessel, the only type that is really called a ship. It is presently being used as a target for bombing practice by the planes of the Royal Army Air Force and she remains indestructible.

The H.M.S. Nubian is listed as number four on the casualty list of the Sixth Flotilla because number three is H.M.S. Zulu, which strikes a mine, resulting in her stern being blown off. She is beached at Gravelines (pronounced Gravlins); a village on the north coast of France. The Straits of Dover are now flowing between the two halves of these destroyers. After the navy's losses of destroyers, a better type of vessel is sent from the Grand Fleet as their replacements.

These ships are of the "L" class that have earned distinguished honors for their role in the Battle of Jutland. They are not the latest models (according to the opinion of other people) but these are cast-offs from the Grand Fleet. While they are a part of the Sixth Flotilla, I do not recall their taking part in any sort of a splash. They are classified according to the first letter of names, such as; Loyal and Lionel. After a brief stay they are replaced by the next later model; the "M" class. Added to them are some from the "N" class.

For all that matters, it does not improve the lot of the destroyers of the Tribal Class. As the H.M.S. Cossack, in trying to make the entrance to Dover Harbour by dead reckoning in the thick of fog, rams the concrete breakwater, thereby pushing her stem back to the bridge and killing all hands on the forecastle head. This accident is reported to be the twenty-second one in number.

The men of the Cossack, at the time of impact, had been standing at attention as a salute to the Flagship that is moored to the first buoy, just inside the Dover Harbour. Like all the other vessels that met disaster, she remains afloat but the condition she is in as a result of this crash clearly indicates that article sixteen of the Rule of the Road at Sea has been totally ignored. Or is the one in charge attempting to go one better than the daring Commander of the Crusader, who would enter the Harbour at high speed toward the mooring buoy, ring full speed astern on approaching it and only then a man would jump onto it on orders from the bridge. Ofttimes the jumper would miss, ending up in the drink, yet never does this ship have the stem ripped like some of the others who try to copy this feat of maneuvers.

The daring Commander is a tall, handsome, athletic type of man who breaks Naval tradition by wearing his hat at a rake upon his head. He also would lose his seniority by fraternizing with the men by swimming with them and indulging in a little horse-play. He had been the navigating officer on a ship that went to the Antarctic at the time the leader of that expedition dies. Many a crewman swallowed hard with his antics.

On the night of November fifth, (a matter of ten days after the Nubian was lost) enemy destroyers stage another raid; being challenged this time by a torpedo boat, the H.M.S. Flirt, that puts its searchlight into play. The light is immediately extinguished by a German shell and following that direct hit, not a trace of her is ever seen again.

Our relief ship is put out of commission during the incident and the enemy flotilla gets to return to its home base unscathed, because of meeting no opposition. Lo and behold, this is the extent of protection for the Straits of Dover. All this happens on a day that is traditionally celebrated with displays of fireworks; to commemorate Guy Fawkes Day, when he is burned in effigy each year for his Gunpowder Plot against the King in the year, 1605.

The first raid (when the Nubian is lost) and the next raid (when the Flirt is destroyed) causes much concerned pressure to be applied to the navy; making the top ones to re-think their strategic deployment. The two raids in a short period of time bring a change in the schedule. At night there is to be no patrol in the Straits; that the vessels in the English half are to anchor in the Downs or at Dungeness, according to the weather conditions; whereas the other half is to anchor off Gravelines or go into Dunkirk.

Although this leaves the Straits unwatched at night, it turns out to be effective in a small way; in that the submarines are more daring and must have thought there is nothing to stop them. One morning in December after having left Dunkirk to resume the regular patrol, objects are sighted that turns out to be German hand-grenades in two cases; and one of the Drifters picks up two bodies who are from a submarine.

For three months we have the comfort for being in the safety of a port at night. Then once more our ship goes into dock for boiler cleaning and to have the guns changed to anti-craft with a two-pound pompom added. Once more I am deprived of leave for the usual reason of having no home; brought about by the fact that the cockney had left, being given command of a minesweeper. After a fortnight we once more go about the business of patrolling the Straits both day and night. We are now equipped to fight off Zeppelins before they reach their Motherland.

The first night is clear and calm with a moon shining through a haze. The haze makes these conditions very unsuitable for searchlights to pick out aircraft, with Boulogne (at this same time) getting a heavy bombing. When the raid has been over for a short time there looms immediately above us, a Zeppelin flying at a low altitude, apparently trying to get its own bearing from the Goodwin Sand Lightship.

The order given by the Action Station is passed along to each man who is turned in for sleep, by the man who had ordered me to make twenty cigarettes each day for him. The manner in which he executes the order is done in the most cunning way. He goes to each individual, touching him lightly and in a voice not much above a whisper, he would say, "Action Station, there's a Zep overhead."

He is asked why he is so quiet issuing the order and the reply is, "It is so low that one could hit it with a piece of coal and I do not want the crew above to hear me."

Looking upward upon reaching the deck, the drone of the propellers is plainly audible and the object is like a cloud silhouetted against the sky. All hands are at their stations waiting for the order to fire; three guns pointing to a target that is practically impossible to miss. The gun crews whisper about the thirty-two pounders that are within the grasp of each one; but alas, the order to fire never comes. The gunner on the foc'sle-head asks this Naval Officer in charge for permission to fire but it is not granted.

When the Goodwin Sands Lightship is spotted, the Zeppelin zooms skyward to live again to spew death and destruction on innocent victims, such as we have seen at Boulogne-sur-Mer (the full name of France's northern coastal seaport on the English Channel). The soft speaking Officer is not asked his reason for not giving the order but volunteers it himself by saying, "It could have bombed us." It happens on February 17, 1917. That could be true if it had any bombs left, after spending the time it did over that French city. This person in charge of us has his wife and children in Dover, a town that has been visited by Zeppelins. How much does he consider them when he lets something like this get away?

Many men in the Drifter Patrol, including the H.M.S. Fletcher's crew, have their families brought from their hometowns to Dover because of their apparent permanent duty being there. Luckily, all these men of the vessels under his command are not present at this display of his cowardice. The men are mostly fishermen and are not in the least interested in knowing the difference of rank between an Admiral and a deckhand. It is what is in the clothes that matter to them. That may have accounted for their own lack of interest in the uniforms they wear. Many have moustaches and wear the black silk kerchief tied around the neck and go on liberty without the blue-collar edged with white tape. Passing commissioned officers on the street does not warrant a salute but these men are doing a real job in most uncomfortably dangerous conditions and recognized for it by their receiving what is commonly termed, "Hard Laying Money."

The man who called us to action in the most considerate, polite way is a quiet person at all times; walking softly where men are sleeping also very inoffensive yet bitter toward authority. One later day while he is at the wheel, the Commander asks him, "Which in your opinion is the better Navy, the British or German?"

The reply is not to the liking of the Old Man, when he comes out with, "If the German Navy offered more money than what I am getting in this one, I would join it."

Then the Commander says a statement, making the quiet Officer eat his own words. "You are not patriotic," the Old Man accuses and then remarks, "One week after you were called to take part, patriotism left you and from that time you thought of nothing but your own safety." There is nothing seditious in the statements to make this Officer offended, but even if there is, it also must remind him of the previous Zeppelin escapade.

The cause of this man's bitterness toward authority is due to his being refused a leave to visit his dying wife in 1914. The only reason given for the denial was, "This Is War." She died and was buried without his being present. That, without doubt, would have left the impression among the relatives that there was a lack of sincerity on his part. His feelings over his loss are indiscernible because he keeps them under control by displaying interest in two rather unusual hobbies. One is learning to play the tin whistle in a remote corner of the fidley, so as to avoid annoying anyone. Regardless of how well he plays, his entertaining is done there to an unseen audience of perhaps two at the most, at one time. His theme song is, "Mary of Argyll." Ofttimes during the day he could be heard softly singing it, though he is not a Scotsman. He is from Liverpool with a dialect that is not heard in any other part of the country; where the letter "G" in the word "sing" is pronounced nearly as hard-sounding as a "K". Imagine hearing the first line sounding as; "I have heard the Mavis sinkink its love sonk to the Morn," and compare it with the way a countryman of Mary would sing that line. The question is could they blend?

His other hobby is the study of explosives by taking the projectile of a six pounder ammunition from the shell case, then setting fire to the stick of cordite after extraction. The projectile is time-fused shrapnel that he has to throw overboard because he cannot take it apart. The shell case is given to a leading seaman gunner who makes cigarette lighters from them.

By way of keeping me occupied, he introduces me to macramé by showing me how three of the simplest knots could produce very artistic patterns. It catches on by many of the crew working together, first to supply a fringe for a mantle-piece. In this way, by the time the next leave comes up, we have a deep fringe six feet long to take home. Into each fringe has been put many hours of labor, by the only one who has no home. It is gratifying to experience the pleasure it gives me. Each one is carefully wrapped and put in my ditty bag.

Each payday brings with it the twine for this interesting hobby. That gives the fishermen an idea. Three of them make net braiding needles (from cigar boxes) and kebles (small pieces of wood used to measure the mesh gauges). Three short poles are put together at their ends and shoes forged in the stoke-hold; and so a small beam-trawl is in the making. Herewith, another hobby is learned without knowing that someday I would use it as a means of my livelihood.

If fish can be caught by net, in all probability they would be attracted to the pretty twine that we use in its construction. This twine comes in four colours; red, blue, green and brown, in glazed-cotton, three-strand eighteen thread count.

In a few days a seventeen beam-trawl is lowered over the port quarter, being towed with only one engine running slowly for one hour; then it is hauled up, mostly out of curiosity. Lo and behold, there appears a bag of thick brill (an edible flatfish) and turbot. This fish have not been disturbed in three years so they are large for these species. The (fishing) stunt could only be pulled off on days when the weather is not suitable for the blimp or the observation balloon to do their submarine spotting. There are times when a good meal is to be had, that is, when the weather behaves for us and in the event one good meal could be spotted.

In being directed to that spot, a depth charge is dropped that would bring a lot of whiting to the surface. When this is done with such satisfactory results it becomes routine to drop one depth charge on the first day of each month but not solely for that purpose. The first type of depth charge consists of an aerial bomb with eighty feet of line attached. On the other end of the aerial bomb we put a float filled with air to function in a way that when the object is dumped, the line becomes taut and releases a pin at the same time to detonate the thing.

One time we send down a depth charge. Fifteen minutes pass without a sound or even a ripple on the water; then the float is hauled aboard and the bomb is towed for a half hour, without any action. It then is brought up to ascertain its problem What happened is that it had blown a hole in one part of it.

In support of the Barrage Patrol some "P" boats were added. This type of craft (when seen from a long distance) resembles a surfaced submarine; equipped with torpedo tubes, guns and six depth charge cradles on the stern that slopes downward. During the same moon period when the Boulogne air-raid was staged, a Zeppelin commanded by the nicest man in the German Air Force came over the Straits.

Of course, being night-time and also being up in the air at a high altitude, the Zeppelin is not visible to us. However, it is in what he does that puts him in that category of being a nice man. Between our ship and a "P" boat that is about two miles away, we drop twenty-two bombs in a direct line. This alerts the shore batteries that send a barrage (ship) accompanied with the bright beams of searchlights to scan the sky. When the Zeppelin is spotted, three quick rounds are fired from the "P" boat in a direct line to the Zep. In the short space of time that it remains visible, we are not even ordered to our stations. The conclusion that can be drawn from this episode is that the Zeppelin Commander either had a conscience or was like our well mannered, whispering "Old Man."

It is on a "P" boat that I witness the shortest stint of service that could ever be performed. Reflecting back to the start at sea that I had made, I could have been rubbed out within an hour of my first day, but it cannot be compared with this incident. The time is Saturday, early afternoon, when the H.M.S. Pinnace pulls alongside a "P" boat moored at the next buoy from the Fletcher. A new crewmember must have just completed his basic training (judging by his kit) is delivered. He and his belongings are put aboard. The Pinnace then takes off to deliver young men to other vessels farther out in the harbour.

The young man is standing on deck waiting, not knowing what to do because there is no one there to direct him. At this time of day in the week at least half of the crew is ashore on liberty and weekend leave. After sauntering around a little while he decides to sit. Where he sits depicts a clear case of laxity or neglect. For reasons of safety to other ships, the depth charges have been removed from their cradles. This lad takes advantage by sitting on one and must have put his foot on the compressed air-valve for throwing the charge. He is literally and instantly blown up to a size. While in the air his uniform rips apart and scatters, he being instantly killed. This must have been seen by the coxswain of the Pinnace that is coming back after completing its mission, to return to the mooring at the end of the pier. The lifeless lad is pulled out of the water. The Pinnace pulls alongside the "P" boat again to get the boy's belongings but in order to do so, the whistle is blown to attract the attention of those on board who are all below and totally unaware of the entire proceedings. This casualty most likely would be listed as "killed in action;" when in reality it was the lack of it.

There are three "P" boats based here. On one of them is a brother to one of our men who comes aboard to visit and tells of a senseless antic of his Commander. As a past-time he would have practice drills of Action Stations and the last man to hit the deck would be punished by having leave stopped and being given extra work. The companion-ways on this type of ship are nothing more than single manholes, so there has to be a last man every time. The ship is not that big that he is not familiar with this condition, therefore it is a case of over-exercising of authority. With that kind of attitude he could rest assured that he could not depend on being rescued by his men if that emergency arose. There are instances where undesirable officers are transferred to the Adriatic and they never reach their destination due to being reported as "Lost At Sea," for the upkeep of morale.

During the war year of 1917 there were only minor problems such as submarines cutting the nets in order to get through the Straits undetected but one day a different technique was used. Instead of cutting the nets, a low flying plane was used to sink the buoys with machine-gun fire. The first attempt was a failure so it was not repeated. On this attempt the plane came down in the water. The cause was not known. However, it surfaced on the side of the nets that prevented the Yacht on patrol from reaching it. Then a Drifter was assigned to retrieve it because of the shallower draft. The plane was taken in tow; the two flyers put aboard and the Drifter set its course towards Dover. When the Yacht's Old Man could see that he was not to get the distinction of delivering his booty, he orders the plane to be sunk by gun-fire and to be added to Davy Jones's locker.

An escort (two blue-jackets) armed with fixed bayonets was waiting on the pier when the Drifter arrived with the two captured pilots, to escort them along the Dover promenade to the Submarine Basin. No one showed signs of hostility toward them, when planes up to this time had not been used for heavy bombing.

Aviation at this time is still in its infancy. Yet the courage of those pilots who fly those planes, regardless of whose side they fight, deserve the highest praise. Air combats are fought with equal numbers on each side. For instances, eight Fokkars attempted to make a daylight raid on Dover; when seven Handley Paige and one Moth went into the air after them. The Moth flew above and went into a tailspin, scattering the group to avoid colliding. When two Fokkars are brought down, the others took off. There are many more planes stationed here that could have been sent up after the six German planes but no, Old Chap, that would not be Cricket.

Another instance is when each Sunday a lone Taube would make a raid at lunchtime, no doubt for the purpose of harassment. On such an occasion a Lieutenant Commander of the Royal Naval Air Service jumped into his seaplane to go after the nuisance. He brought it down, just one on one. For this deed he is court-martialed on two accounts-disobeying (no) orders, also being out of uniform. Was he just simply showing off or did his conscience tell him to stop this live danger? Surely he recognized his own mortality as a viable option.

7

Channel raids, the cure, the price

To my recollection there were no more raids of any disastrous consequence through the remainder of 1917. Shortly later, on the night of February fourteenth of the next year, one raid was staged by a flotilla of enemy destroyers, whereby they had shown their utter contempt for the Dover Patrol. On this specific night what was the Dover Patrol especially doing? The answer to the question, rest assured, would not be truthfully given by anyone in a superior position in a military office ashore. For that matter very few, if any, would be of a veracious nature.

For example, take apart an incident from the Battle of Jutland, when a fifteen-year-old boy is awarded the highest decoration of service, for staying on his post at a gun when all the rest of the gun's crew had been killed. His picture and the propaganda that went with it were in the newspapers. Even if this was true, should not the country feel ashamed to use boys of this age for most dastardly experiences? I think so. This served the enemy better (propaganda-wise) than it did for his own country. Although he received the highest honor, he was very dead when he got it. Regardless of what any lower-deck rating had ever done in the way of bravery during wartime, no Victoria Cross was ever awarded to a living one; that is, up to and past that time.

It is the night of St. Valentine when love is supposed to rule. The Straits, a stretch of twenty-one miles between shores, had on its surface sixty-three drifters, also one yacht as parent ship to half of them and a steam-trawler assigned to the Yacht Patrol to be mother to the other half. Every seventh drifter had wireless so that left fifty-four without. During the night a flotilla of enemy destroyers, playing their searchlights on England's first line of defense, the Drifter Patrol, put every one of the wireless equipped vessels out of commission. They finished the attack by sinking a Paddle Minesweeper that also had wireless. This was performed in such a short space of time that it is doubtful, due to the element of surprise, a signal of any nature was sent out. Was it coincidental that all the vessels equipped with wireless were primarily targeted?

This happened on the night prior to our having to go on patrol and while we were in the Dover Harbour on shore leave until ten o'clock. On nights such as that, the wireless telegraphist upon returning aboard, would automatically go to his shack before turning in, to put on the headphones to listen to unusual happenings. He heard nothing important or he would have informed us.

The next morning the "Old Man" gave orders to the effect that we were to go out to tell all ships in the Patrol to return to Dover, because there had been no communication from them. Some were already on the way back with their wounded while those who had not been attacked were informed by megaphone. This task took a few hours to perform by a ship with twin-engines that could do no more than nine and one-half knots an hour in war and peace times.

When all ships were back, sometime between four and five in the afternoon of the next day of February 15, 1918, then the Commander went ashore for further orders. In the meantime the Dover Straits are totally void of armed vessels and meaning that we are not replaced by any of the destroyers weighing anchor in the Dover Harbour. After a short space of time the Old Man returns with the most contemptuous orders, saying, "All ships in the Drifter Patrol go back to sea and resume patrol!" Were all the anchored destroyers on leave or down time?

Upon reflection, one wonders how many of the English populace knew that on this night they were to get double protection from the mighty Armada of small wooden ships, manned by iron-men who were sitting ducks. She had something laughable on deck with which would be a waste of time and life to attempt to challenge any enemy. War craft like what had decimated our ranks the previous night would soon know that the weaponry was as false as the sitting ducks. Such talk was the topic of conversation in the Wardroom on the H.M.S. James Fletcher as the ship proceeded to its favourite and accustomed hunting-grounds.

The Commander soon related the experiences of some of the Skippers who had lived through hell on the night before. When they were asked what type of ships they were using, one of them went to the Captain's office window of the Drifter Patrol, (overlooking the harbour) and said, "None to compare with what we saw last night." Could it have been the reason they were not sent? From it, a plan of strategy was conceived that the only course of action to take in the event of a repetition of the great naval battle that was (un) fought was that every man should have a lifebelt very close to him at all times. In that regard we had all been lax yet at the same time no attempt was to be made to fire back with our heaviest armament: the six-pounder. Henceforth, there would not be piped, "Action Station."

The Skippers were asked by the Captain, "Did you fire at them?"

The answer, "What the hell with?"

It took only one shell to knock out each vessel and the one that hit our relief went right through the Lieutenant's head before exploding. He was one I knew who frequented the Grand Hotel when I was employed there. He was a gentleman. The information of the event that I could pass along was sketchy; that is, repeating what the Commander got to know in the short time he was ashore.

The topic of conversation among the crew was in effect how good are our defenses? There was the six-inch gun on the breakwater that did not fire at the enemy flotilla with their glaring searchlights and guns blazing. About eighteen months earlier another similar gun was not fired when the raid was made and the Nubian was torpedoed. Was this gun made of the same material as the one placed in a city in the Northeast of England, when a Zeppelin severely bombed it? After the raid some of the residents of that port went to investigate as to the reason it had not fired and found that it was made of wood. Needless to say it was dismounted in quick time so as never to fire again, as if it ever did or could.

Late one night after resuming our assigned patrol, the seaman who did not want to alert the Commander of the Zeppelin by shouting the order, "Action Stations!" came below to tell us in his usual cool manner, "Get your lifebelts on, they're here again." We instantly darkened the quarters and opened the skylight to be used as an exit-hatch for some (usually for the young ones) in an emergency, while our messenger went to the Chief Engineer via the companion-way.

While this matter was being discussed in hushed tones amongst us, immediately overhead appeared a bright light. It was a Zeppelin's searchlight. We watched through the open skylight while, one by one, six German destroyers were passing by without firing a shot. What a relief it was to see them go down the line of the doubled Armada with nothing more to throw at us than a beam of light. Tension was not completely diminished because we feared that the fireworks were being saved for the return trip to their bases in Ostende or Zeebrugge. Yet when the end of the line had been reached a few token salvoes from the Zeppelin were fired into Dover. It brought a measure of relief knowing that they, in this case, should not have to be referred to as our immediate enemies because they would have to take a direct course homeward which was a few miles farther North.

Undoubtedly, their action was a direct challenge for the contempt shown to them when a mosquito-fleet was sent to accompany a beautiful lady (fully manned and equipped warship) in order to uphold a naval country's tradition. Upon occasion when upset, the ship could make the surface of the water go very uneven. Did she rule the waves on this night? No! How easy it would be for those enemy destroyers to repeat the Valentine's Day performance? Yet they did not. When all danger had passed there ensued a discussion as to the reason for our being spared. The practical theory was to save their ammunition in the event of a conflict. There were some of us who credited the good fortune of our being spared by our having on board the bunting-tosser who had missed two prior close calls.

Two days later a mine was sighted, one from our own minefields yet a different kind from those we had been using to sink with rifle fire. This type would not explode when filled with holes to make it sink. Consequently, approaching this one in the usual manner (by getting close before open firing) would produce slightly different results. One half dozen rifles were aimed at the object and on a command were simultaneously fired. There followed an explosion causing the ship to lurch to starboard. I had been watching this target practice from below deck, by standing on a drop folding-seat and looking through a port when it exploded. I was hurled across to the other side. Picking myself up, thinking that nothing had happened until I saw blood on the floor, Looking for its source, I found one end of my left index finger was hanging off. At the time of the blast my hands were on the pantry table for support; not using a knife at the time. I had my right hand across the handle of it. It was still in my hand when I gathered myself.

Then followed as pretty a piece of first-aid that one will ever see. This work was always left to the ship's steward, such as the time when the barrels of rum were being hauled aboard. One of the signal boys sustained a deep gash in the palm of his left hand as he was trying to steady the barrels from hitting the deck-housing. Later that day a destroyer was sighted with a doctor on board. It came alongside. The injury was checked and redressed, with the doctor commending the steward for his treatment.

In my case, a Lieutenant took my injury out of our Steward's hands by giving the impression that he knew what to do. He requested a needle and thread; the same was supplied. He pushed this through the end of my hanging digit before coming to the conclusion that he could not complete the stitching unless he went halfway down my finger; so he took the thread out. His next step was to hand me over to the Steward and absolutely refusing to be responsible for the outcome. The Steward was to bind my finger tightly with adhesive tape and bandage it.

Later, the pain was most intense. My hand swelled and the night was spent pacing the deck.

The next morning a motor launch was sighted and signaled to come alongside to take me into Dover sickbay. Before that could be done this motor launch had a mission to accomplish; in the nature of picking up five mines that had washed ashore at Dungeness. Eventually the point was reached. The skipper of the motor launch was a young submarine Lieutenant of the Royal Navy Volunteer Reserve and in navy circles referred to as Harry Tates' Navy. The real Harry Tate was the country's leading comedian. This was not to discredit the ability of the young lads who served in this department, but because they had been trained at the Crystal Palace; a theatre in London that had been commandeered for the purpose. Wireless telegraphists were also trained there and each month on the James Fletcher a new one came to receive on the job training from a much experienced Chief Petty Officer.

Upon sighting the five objects, this young skipper pointed her bow to the shore as close as safely possible to them, but they were still a few yards farther inshore, as it was low-tide. This was the first mission of its kind for this crew. I was asked if I had any experience in handling mines. Yes, I was able to provide them with information that put their fears to rest. I went to one, put my finger (the right index one because my left one was still out of commission) on one of the detonators.

"Provided this is not hit with something equaling forty pounds of pressure, they are safe," I informed my spectators.

Then we went about the task of retrieving the five mines, by sliding a boat hook handle through the ring located at the top of each sphere. Two of us, one on each side of every mine, carried the respected thing to the boat for the young skipper to lash and stow.

Being occupied in this way helped me from feeling the pain in my left hand. Now we are finally Dover bound. By the time we reach there, the sickbay for the men of the Dover Patrol is closed for the day. This means it would be another night without treatment. Ofttimes I since have wondered, that if the war was to be conducted this way; why shouldn't men be wounded only during the daytime hours? Pity, it is, to inconvenience those poor chaps operating in the sickbay. They were only in an environment resembling maritime conditions-where rain fell on their windows overlooking the harbour, not shells.

The next morning I attended the sickbay. An orderly removed the bandage and what he saw brought out a burst of laughter. It brought the doctor over to see the joke. The nail on my finger was facing in nearly the opposite direction. The adhesive was removed, the finger tip repositioned, the hand bandaged and I was to be back at one-thirty to board the Ambulance for the Royal Marine's Hospital at Deal, a distance of nine miles.

There were two of us on this day to make the trip. The other one was a Royal Naval Air Service man who had survived an extensive and severe bombing raid in Northern France and who had absolutely no control of any part of his body due to shell-shock. Having arrived at the hospital, the regulation treatment began with a bath, a dose of quinine and two nine-point-twos for bowel behaviour. These last pills got their name from Navy men because of their size in corresponding with a large gun that fired a projectile with a diameter of nine-point-two inches. Then I went on, to a ward with twenty beds. I take the only vacancy, next to a lad who at eighteen has spent three and a half years in this hospital, recovering from a wound on his shin that absolutely refused to heal.

At the outbreak of the war at the age of fourteen, he was in the Yeomanry, a reserve cavalry regiment. He was sent to France but soon after arriving at the front with the introduction of barbed-wire entanglements, cavalry could not be used. He was assigned to tend the horses while his regiment went to the front as infantry. An enemy artillery shell hit an ammunition-dump close by, killing and wounding a number of the animals and that is when he got hit. He was many miles from home in this hospital and the only army casualty in this ward, at least by his own request. His reasoning in this matter is most unselfish. The nearest Military Hospital to his home was so far away that his mother would be hard-pressed for time and money to visit him. He kept the distance in order to make it practically impossible for her to visit but he would write to her each day.

In this ward were also four casualties of the Channel raid made on the night of St. Valentine's Day; three from the Paddle-Minesweeper and a Skipper of a Drifter. This man was previously the one who had learned wireless telegraphy. His ship got a shell in the wheelhouse that burst, hitting him in the face, taking off the left side of it, including the eye, one buttock, two fingers and a fractured leg from shrapnel. He was fifty-five years of age.

When a pretty nurse with red hair dressed his wounds, her eyes would fill with tears, for the admiration of this man who would not emit even a murmur as she tended him. This was brought to the attention of those higher up so that on the following day the First Sea Lord, accompanied by his wife, visited this man to inform him that His Majesty would pay him a visit on the Thursday following.

During those few moments his wife struck up a conversation with the man in the next bed, saying, "It was a fine scrap you put up." The reply to that did not seem to her liking, because she beat a hasty retreat into the hall.

In the clear tones of a Scotsman came, "Aye, it werrre all on one side, the oth-errr."

After one week in bed this Skipper insisted on being allowed to be up in a wheelchair to enjoy the company of his wife and daughter who were allowed as many hours as they wished during the day. They would take him on the grounds but on this Thursday he was asked to stay in bed until the King's visit. In the afternoon, His Majesty, King George V, made a trip, especially to decorate this man with the Distinguished Service Cross. We, the ambulatory patients, were ordered to stand at attention at the foot of his bed. His Majesty circled the room, leaving without a word other than wishing this man a speedy recovery. He had the appearance of being under a great strain and looked much older than forty-nine.

For what reason had this man been decorated when by his own admission he had done nothing to warrant it? He had been in a wrong place at the right time. Therefore, he did not attach any value to it. It would not bring back his eye. It was for his exceptional behaviour in the hospital, that was vastly different from that of the man in the next bed to him; the one who had given the snappy answer to the wife of the First Sea Lord. The nurse would barely enter the ward to dress wounds when this man would start hollering from pain not yet inflicted and every man in the ward would join him.

After my finding out what ship the Skipper was from, I reminded him of an incident in which he was not their skipper but a participant; one that might have had repercussions had it not been for his cool head and a lot of luck Although our ship was a twin-screw it was not that fast. The skipper of the smaller vessel, when the opportunity availed itself, would race with us. On the day in mind, a stiff breeze from the east was blowing directly onto the Kentish coast, accompanied by a fairly rough sea, when the patrol weighed anchor to proceed to Dover from the Downs; a distance of nine miles. This skipper's drifter was to windward of us but had a gaff mainsail, always called the mizzen. As we kept on the same course, she was making more leeway than we. By the time both ships were nearing the harbour entrance we were so close to each other that when one of us was on the crest of a wave, the other was starting at the ebbing of that one while at the same time all crewmen were hanging onto something for dear life. It was a most harrowing experience for a short while and to think that a collision could be effected in such a manner, as one vessel jumping on the top of another. Just as the entrance was reached we touched broadside without a splinter being knocked off the wooden hull of the drifter.

The Skipper now agreed with me (after being reminded) that it was a little too close for comfort, but also knowing that to alter course in these conditions would have been disastrous, because the sterns of each ship would collide. Following our discussion of that incident, I told him of the protest staged by the wives of the crewmen of the Drifter Patrol, outside the Admiral's Office and about the events of the following night, including the interview of the two racing skippers in the Captain's Office of the Drifter Patrol.

A week after my admission to the hospital I was scheduled for an operation on the following day. The ward orderly gave me this information and he told me what would be done. He seemed quite knowledgeable in such matters, saying that the severed tendon would be knotted but it would not hold. During his study of medicine he had let his drinking get the upper-hand, forcing him to quit his studies to become a ward orderly. The day following the operation with my finger bent, the nurse upon dressing it told me to straighten it. Swollen with five stitches in it, she forced it straight and from that moment on it never bent again.

A fortnight later it was time to discharge me at the doctor's discretion. With my having had an operation it was for him to recommend that number of days leave to be granted; usually between seven and twenty-one, depending on the nature of it. He came to me with the same line that I had heard every three months during my nearly two years of service.

"The records show you have no home and no next of kin, so there is no need to recommend you for leave."

In reply I repeated what the cockney Lieutenant had said, "Sir, I would like to see the sights of London."

On hearing this he apologized. The sickbay treatment I had received called for seven days leave. He extended the recommendation to ten days, saying that was not enough time to see all the sights. "Enjoy yourself, young sailor," he added.

Next day I rejoined the ship and presented this recommendation to the Commander who immediately turned it down for the reason that had been given so many times before. The Steward had a seaman assisting him during my absence, asked me if the leave was granted so that he would know how much longer he would have the services of this man.

In disgust I said, "By Christ, if I ever have a son who joins the Navy without next of kin, I'll tell him to first make some."

This was the punishment inflicted upon one who had somehow sinned against British society. Judged, but not directly being told that I was an unwanted off-spring of an erring couple, seemed to be the concord. Paupers' Mansion would never let me think otherwise or allow me to forget their judgment. I hoped that when my time came to live in an adult world, things would change. Not so, but why not? Then, this may be the interpretation of the quotation in the Bible, "The sins of the father shall be visited unto the children." All of us who had spent years in the Dover Union Institution in similar circumstances are to be blamed? Punished for any wrongs done against society, as these snobs who went around with utter distain towards us. Is this what they would have us believe? At least there was some consolation in knowing that although His Majesty did not speak when he saw me in the hospital-ward; he did not look at me in any way different from the way he looked at the others.

One night a few weeks later, Sparks, after having spent the evening ashore, went to the wireless shack right away, as usual. Standing outside with the headphones on, he told us that something is going on outside and that two flotilla leaders were being ordered to return to Dover. All patrolling by night had been canceled following the second raid, so that these two ships were on their way to Dunkirk when this signal was sent. No ships left the harbour and the details were sketchy as to what action was taking place. The next morning at seven o'clock one of the two ships went to its mooring-buoy with a few bodies on the quarter-deck draped with the Union Jack. A few hours later a signal was sent to all ships containing the order, "Dress ship and splice the main brace," as the other flotilla leader was appearing and having to be towed in by a destroyer that has been ordered out to sea for this purpose.

Word spread throughout the town. People flocked to the promenade. All ships lined their riggings, superstructures and decks with their crews in compliance of the order, as the second flotilla leader was being towed to its mooring-buoy. Then a most dramatic event took place as some members of the crew of this disabled ship stood at attention with fixed bayonets and rifles, as a cutter pulled alongside to take prisoners to the Naval Pier. Captured in a hand-to-hand battle, they numbered twenty-nine altogether. As they stood there a speech was made to them for the heroic part they played. Then upon a command, they sprang to attention and were marched between the armed blue jackets with shouldered-arms and fixed bayonets glistening in the sun. As they marched along the street crowded with people, there was not a sign of hostility displayed by anyone. It was a most impressive, unforgettable sight. The details of the event were disclosed by the crews of the two ships that routed six of the enemy ships in this manner. They were given shore leave. So off to the pubs many went, entering the establishments with the names of their ships on their caps in gold letters; either H.M.S. Swift or H.M.S. Broke. After a few pints of a popular British brew had been poured down many hatches, this unique Naval battle was verbally re-enacted, not in a boastful manner by what had been accomplished but in a hostile way as though each crew was responsible for the actions of their Commanding Officers.

To begin with, it was a chance meeting that these two ships should encounter the German flotilla. The action began with the Broke disabling one ship then leaving it to engage with another ship. While doing so, the Swift finishes off the first one that is disabled by the Broke. The Broke disables another ship and in the engagement, she is disabled, too. She is hit in the stokehold that bursts one of the main steam pipes, killing twenty-seven men. Regardless, the Commander calls for full-speed that is reduced to being quite slow. However, he heads his ship to ram the one that is crippled but he could barely dent it. Then his men scramble onto the fo'c'sle head to face off with the crew on the opposing ship.

Their purpose was to fight, evidently, because in the encounter one of the midshipmen loses an eye. Now the question is, "Who is so daringly commanding our flotilla leader-ship?" Lo and behold! He is that tall, good-looking man who wears his cap at an angle in defiance of British Navy regulations, who holds every-one spellbound for the way he would bring the H.M.S. Crusader to her mooring buoy and yet never put a dent in her. He advertises in his bearing that he is fear-less. Surely he proves it when he has the courage to engage in combat while being outnumbered three to one. His original order had been to return to Dover but no ships went from Dover to him.

The time allotted for beer-drinking according to the law has expired but the heated argument between the two ships' companies continues as they walk the narrow street that has the most pubs, eating-houses and shops of any street in the town. Among the shops are green-grocers with stands on the pavement in front, full of what appears to be vegetables to some, but on this day it is considered as ammunition. The crews, taking their positions on each side of the street, pelt each other with the produce. It also nearly becomes a hand-to-hand battle because this particular street is very narrow, like so many in the old historic towns of England. This engagement lasted as long as the owner brought in the produce. When the ammunition supply was depleted, orders were sent to other shops to leave nothing outside. The pelting soon stopped.

There is a sad side to this story regarding the casualties. Whereas, the march-ing of the captured men may have been staged to boost the morale of the people ashore, it may have been deemed inappropriate to follow that with a funeral pro-cession of a like number of the dead. Nothing of that sort took place, but why would our dead not be entitled to this honour? I sadly wondered, then and for years later. It should be mentioned how they were killed without a remote chance of escape. Their bodies were not brought ashore in full view and it could be presumed that they were taken back to where their end had come; in Davy Jones's locker, en masse. The night following that engagement was not repeated as of St. Valentine's Day but the same conditions prevailed. Not a ship left the harbour, even ones with speed of over thirty knots an hour, to meet an enemy in a twenty-mile stretch of water. Had the words of the two skippers influenced the Admiral when told by them that there was nothing in our harbour that could compare to their class? That may have been the case.

About a month later, on the evening of April twenty-second, a destroyer with flags flying and spelling out the words, "St. George and England forever," left Dover Harbour. She was in a convoy to begin something that was not directly made public to civilians-other than to nine hundred marines who had volunteered for it. Each one received one month's leave with one month's pay in advance prior to their going. The next morning we awoke to find an old cruiser moored to the next buoy. She was stripped of armament with not a sign of life aboard. Upon looking closer she bore evidence of very much death as she laid there, bullet riddled and blood spattered from end to end. These men had been used as decoys while an attempt was made to stop enemy destroyers from leaving Zeebrugge and Ostende by torpedoing the lock-gates with two American built motorboats having speeds of about forty-five knots. This was successful. Consequently, old cruisers were scuttled to block the channel to the harbour's entrance. This was done with little or if any loss of life and most certainly was sufficient to stop the Channel-Raiders.

The reports in the newspapers of this event did not go into elaborate details glorifying it, other than stating the blocking of the channels, the torpedoing of the lock-gates and seventy-nine men (all there were who made the landing) were taken prisoners. The reward to the leader of this resulting massacre was a Knighthood bestowed on the Admiral of the Dover Patrol by His Majesty King George V.

The H.M.S. Vindictive, following this episode, returned to Dover during the night. So quietly was she moored to the buoy nearest the Fletcher that no one saw or heard any part of it. Upon her discovery a small boat with two crewmen in it from our ship pulled away to ascertain the reason for her being there. The morning was grey. She, like Navy ships, was of a similar color but she lay there like a picture of stark nudity. For one full week she lay moored without a soul having boarded her. Then, during the night of April twenty-ninth, she left as she had come; unheralded, unheard and unseen. The next knowledge of her whereabouts came from the newspapers, stating that she had been scuttled in the channel entrance to Ostende.

In the event that there were nine hundred men aboard her to be used as a decoy landing party, only seventy-nine made it to the Molle of Zeebrugge. There is reason to believe that the rest were casualties, mostly killed, judging by the condition of the ship on its return. But where were the dead? Burials at sea in the past were performed by fire-bars lashed to the corpses before dumping. That would take place on ships that were coal fired for the making of steam. But in this instance there were a lot of dead. Perhaps no fire-bars could be used, as she may have been oil fired and had very little time to clear the decks. What if the whole gory scene was not to be photographed? Taking all these matters into consideration, the most likely and convenient way to dispose of the remains of those young men who had been slaughtered in that way; was to dump them at sea.

Or were they sacrificed to protect the unreasonable excuse of an incident that happened nearly four years previously, when a peasant killed a prince in the Balkans. Would they be dropped below decks, the hatches closed and moor the ship, then abandon her? In that manner there would be nobody around to answer the questions of curiosity seekers. But she was available to photographers at a distance only. The question remains that was she scuttled in the channel? By the time she would arrive at her destination, dawn in all probability would be breaking. She would still be within reach of shore batteries that had not been knocked out by the raid of the week before. Or was she torpedoed on orders from the higher quarters? The answer was not given nor will it ever be made known but there lies the "Unknown Grave of eight hundred twenty-one Soldiers."

Such was the aftermath. It absolutely had nothing whatsoever to do with the prevention of Channel-Raids. It served the purpose to glorify and magnify an incident to satisfy the ego of the perpetrator who was Knighted for this most callous of brain-waves. Therein, lies a reason for a young person to at least hesitate or refuse to take up arms to maim or kill one from another country. Moreover, how could he kill or maim ones from his own country, or in turn, to be maimed or killed?

Regardless, the war continued, as evidenced by the loss of another of the Tribal Class destroyers being towed in, minus the forward half to the foremost funnel. Such was the fate of the H.M.S. Tartar. To offset the loss, a replacement was made by two halves of destroyers being joined into one. The bows of the Zulu were secured to the after-part of the Nubian. Their names combined to be called Zubian.

Of the many destroyers of the Tribal Class that had been knocked out of commission, one man was a survivor of four of them; resulting in his being absolutely
shunned by all blue-jackets as a Jonah. His condition was that of a punch-drunk
fighter who did not study the art of self-defense but it had been bestowed upon
him by a Divine Right. He had a Guardian Angel to watch over him, unlike our
bunting-tosser whose halo covered the entire ship that seemed to be his alone.
Ironically, the name of the survivor from four destroyers was the same as that of
the Assistant to the Assistant Headmaster of the boys in the Union, who took
part in the relief of Antwerp at the age of sixty-three.

About the same time another of the Tribal Class was restored and rejoined the
Sixth Flotilla: the H.M.S. Viking, with her many funnels. The loss of the Nubian
was the only one as a direct result of enemy action, because the Cossack, through
human error-if it can be so classified, and the rest struck mines. But there was one
mishap that was outstanding. It was a beautiful June day late in the afternoon at
the Naval Pier. The Promenade was well populated with men beginning liberty
from the ships in the harbour. Suddenly an explosion occurred. Looking in the
direction from whence it came; men, oil and flames were shooting skyward. It
happened to one of the latest of Monitors that had come from a large munitions
depot. Only that day it was loaded with either fifteen or sixteen-inch shells and to
proceed later to bombard the Belgian coast.

A sort of martial law was put into effect. Troops were called to evacuate the
residents from their houses. Two blocks from the waterfront were more troops
lining that street to prevent others from entering the supposed danger zone. This
was a precautionary action ordered by the Admiral. It was his opinion that in
event the ammunition exploded, it would blow the whole town up because the
white cliffs of Dover had miles of tunneling that stored munitions. Between the
burning ship that was moored just inside the harbour and the houses on shore,
were all the vessels of the entire Dover Patrol, with the exception of the Drifters
on the Barrage Patrol.

The decision was made by the same one who only two months before was
Knighted for his strategy used in the blocking of the ports on the Belgian Coast.
No order was given to have the ship towed to sea. God only knows there were
enough steam-trawlers built for towing purposes. Their crews with their knowledge, combined with their courage, could have completed this maneuver in far
less time than it took the soldiers to muster and march into town to get those
people from their houses. Where under His heaven did this Admiral get his training? Not even in Harry Tates' Navy.

However, as the evening wore on notices appeared on the screens of movie theatres. Announcements were made publicly as to the disposition of this tragic event at intervals of about every half hour. Then at precisely ten o'clock the final announcement came. The H.M.S. Gorgan was torpedoed just where she lay, without stating that the order to abandon ship was given prior to its execution. Is it possible for a witness to such sadistic events relay in writing or by word of mouth without at least developing a lump in the throat? He would be no less a man for allowing tears to stream down his face at the thought of so many young men needlessly, "Sailing into the Valley of Death." That partial quotation (from a well known poet), in instances of this nature is not as fitting as the one of another, "Authority in the hands of a fool is a dangerous weapon."

The depth of water where she was sunk was far less than the length of the beam of the ship. She was torpedoed on one side-that was the one side resting on the bottom, with plenty of the other part showing. At the same time she was obstructing the entrance to the harbour at one end of the breakwater. In the first place, it is doubtful that she was needed for the purpose intended because the news coming from the Western Front at this time was encouraging and channel-raids had ceased. The only menace left were submarines and they were the problem for the Drifter Patrol to solve.

One very good move that was made in solving the submarine menace was done by mine-layers in the following manner. Two passenger ships commissioned for this purpose would cross the Straits with one being slightly ahead. Each one dropping twenty mines then pausing for a short distance before dropping twenty more and so on. If one of the mines broke adrift and was exploded by rifle fire or if something submerged to cause a detonation, then a most unusual sight would be seen. The explosion of one would set off the row of twenty that would cause a hill of water to be formed and most often on the top would be a Drifter as we constantly patrolled over the mine fields. The "no nighttime patrol" order was still in effect. Although there was no fear of channel-raids, our Commander decided to be the exception but it was very short-lived.

For a period of time each month there were two medals issued by the Admiralty to men of ships in the Drifter Patrol. Given not to anyone in particular for outstanding performance, they were accepted in a way similar to their being awarded via the raffle. Later they were cherished to the extent that this hardware was returned. But our Commander was disappointed that none had been thrown in his direction, so he asked for one. The month before he had requested an armchair. That was refused. Now he wanted a medal. With his being a commissioned officer it would be a Distinguished Service Order. He was told to go out and earn it. It was the custom to leave the patrol each day about an hour before darkness set in, but this first day at sea following the denial of a medal, our Commander decided that we alone are going to rule all the waves in the Straits.

It is evening. A stiff breeze is blowing. A few of us are assembled in the galley, discussing the actions of the "Old Man" in his quest for hardware. The wind is off the port-bow so that the side-galley door is closed until the end of the patrol is reached. Then the ship is brought about. The starboard side-door closes. I was nearest the other door and as I reach to open it, the ship lurches. I am thrown to the rail. At that moment I see what I think is a new cork-fender, then as it rears its ugly head above the water I could do nothing more than stand there frozen-with my outstretched arm pointing at a mine that seems close enough for me to touch. Another man seeing it grabs a boat-hook to keep it from making contact. Fortunately the stern passes right over it as the ship comes around. Now it is to windward. When this is brought to the attention of the Commander, he rings full speed ahead towards our assigned anchorage; leaving it to hit or be hit. For the brief spell of one hour he has guarded the Straits of Dover alone.

From that time on nothing of consequence, foolish or otherwise, happened. Then late in September there appeared in one of the London evening papers an article stating that the French Government was giving a special medal with money to the men who served on the Barrage Patrol but the Admiralty refused it. The reason for France doing so was to show their appreciation that between January first and September first, 1918, sixty-three submarines were sunk by our Drifter Patrol. The Admiralty gave no reason for the refusal yet in the Naval Barracks that fact was listed on the wall of Naval tradition. One reason may have been because there would not be one of those medals on any British blue-jacket who had signed for duty after the war begun.

About three weeks later the "flu" began to take its toll and the first to get it on our ship was the carpenter. The day we left Dover he was assigned to erect awning-spars on the bridge. After a few hours he reported sick and was unable to continue. Going to his bunk he nearly collapsed. The Old Man visited the disappointed carpenter who said that all he wanted was to see the Cliffs of Dover.

He was a powerfully built quiet man, not one to argue. He was sick for two days while I catered to him. Then I contracted the epidemic that was sweeping the entire country. I was sick to the point where it was difficult to stand. However, the next day a signal was sent to all ships requesting that all men complaining of not feeling well should be given the benefit of the doubt and be brought in to report to the sickbay.

In the carpenter's case, reporting to the sickbay was entirely out of the question as he was sinking rapidly. He was put on the hospital ship that was moored in the harbour where he stayed alive for just one week. I was one of three crewmen who reported. Upon doing so, I was given one look from a distance by the doctor who immediately assigned a man to escort and assist me to the makeshift hospital. This was an unused boardinghouse, similar to the one used as the sickbay directly across the street. The other two crewmen were just malingerers taking advantage of the situation, nevertheless they were taken by the ambulance to the Royal Marine's Hospital.

Where I was placed was the latest in hospital improvements for the cure of an unknown sickness. Therefore, it was the opinion of the doctor that the cure lays in the victim: being starved in order to drive the germ from one's system. A truer word was never spoken, if the results from his treatment are in any way a criterion. I was next put into a small room with three beds in it. Two were occupied, of course, and the space left permitted the door to open halfway. Enough space to allow an average sized person to enter, providing he was not carrying a tray of food. That puzzled me as to how we could be fed? The solution was not long in coming.

First of all, there was no closet for clothes. The uniform was stowed on the foot of the bed with shoes beneath. How I longed to get into bed with clothes on but that was not permitted. Regardless of my condition I did manage to retain my underwear because no clothing was supplied. It saved time and energy with very little left of the latter.

Late that afternoon the last meal of the day was delivered. Lo and behold, the supper for us three individuals entered the room in the right hand of an orderly, with one finger through the handles of three enameled tin cups containing evaporated milk diluted with water. The treatment for this malady that prevailed was left to the discretion of the doctor. He personally supervised without any outside interference, either from above or below him. A thought grazed my mind. Was this doctor related to the one at Paupers' Mansion?

The other tenants in this room were discussing the conditions of this hotel. One of them had gone two floors down to the basement for a drink of water from a washbasin that was the only water outlet in the entire house. There was no receptacle from which to drink, therefore, the only way was to put one's mouth beneath the spout. The regulations forbade one to leave his bed. It was an all male roster for the purpose of drinking water but it so happened that the other facility was also down there and there was no one around to enforce the rule.

The speaker was the latter of the two who had made the last trip for water. He was relating that he saw an open door on the floor below but could not tell by the position of a patient in the room whether he died getting out of bed or not. Perhaps he was going for water or he succumbed returning because he was kneeling with one hand and head resting on the bed. No charts were kept of the patients. No temperatures, pulses or respirations taken but once each day the doctor made rounds to ask each one how he felt. The answer he received was conclusive, according to the conversation of the sick shipmates. Their strategy was planned for the next visit, to the effect that regardless of their condition, they were both going to tell him that they felt well. They had heard that upon discharge from this domicile, two days at least would be spent on the overflow battleship, H.M.S. Arrogant, where quarters had been set aside as a convalescent-ward for victims recovering from the "flu" and as a precaution in the event of a relapse.

At nine o'clock the following morning the breakfast came in, in the same form as the previous meal. To say the least, my condition physically had not improved but my spirit was buoyed up as the result of hearing this discussion. The next two hours were entertaining as these two were rehearsing their plans of escape from the latest in health spas. At eleven o'clock the doctor came in with the orderly to execute orders given. Sure enough the plan was successful. The men were ordered to wait downstairs at noon for the vehicle to take them to the place of recuperation. Turning to me, asking the usual question, I answered him with enough bluff to convince him that my condition was much improved but had I been ordered to stand he was in a position to tell me that I was a damned liar.

The doctor and orderly continued their rounds. While my two room-mates were getting dressed, one said, "We will be back for you, Shorty, in two days time."

"I will bloody well hold you to it," I replied with disappointment.

They left. Now the room was mine with the expectation of seeing these two vacant beds occupied by two others, as this epidemic had not subsided but that was not to be. The craving for water was uncontrollable. My only means of conveyance to the basement was on all fours and having to go in reverse while descending. My eyes were barely open due to the weight of my head that felt like a ton. The halls were dark even in daytime yet the desire for water reigned uppermost. The challenge of descent had to be overcome without knowing if I would slide or roll downstairs and not much caring.

The first floor was reached. Then while descending the next flight, my foot touches something that feels human, so I roll over into a sitting posture. There is a corpse obstructing my passage. I continue the rest of the way in this position and find it to be less of a strain. On reaching the wash-basin there are five men.

I mention, "There's a man dead on the stairs."

One sick man answers, "Not news, lad, we all had to pass the poor bloke."

While discussing the number of patients who had left this place in this way, another emaciated man speaks, "Heed this, does any one notice, no replacements are coming to fill these beds?"

One in the group adds, "They're making better places to go according to what the orderly says."

Better facilities may have been a cover-up for the high mortality rate of this small institution numbering nine in three weeks. That discouraging news served the purpose of self-determination to survive with the only weapon left—one's constitution.

Returning to the room as a quadruped did not seem as tiring to me as descending from it. Now that a reason for getting out of bed had been found, there was only one other thing to do while lying alone in that room. Plan. Knowing that another day would pass without food or medicine before the doctor would come, I will attempt to look him straight in the eye and tell him that I feel much better today, although I could not stand. If I fail to convince him, then what should I do? Climbing the stairs for a cherished drink of water will be the test of my lessening durability, so it is to "make or break" my endurance. The next morning he came with the usual question. He got the planned lying answer but did not recommend my discharge. He did add that if I showed the same improvement tomorrow he would release me. Another day without a meal, medicine or company in the room, made me want to crawl off. Completely deserted except for the brief visits of the orderly who would serve me a seven-course dinner in a tin-cup without even a napkin.

Ofttimes I wondered how England complied with the message that was sent out at the Battle of Trafalgar? Over one hundred fifteen years past, flags announced: England Expects That Every Man Will Do His Duty. Undoubtedly, the response was good because Lord Nelson managed to infiltrate the fleet of French and Spanish ships or was it just his day with luck?

During the afternoon of my lonely day, without any idea of the time although a watch is on my wrist that has not been wound for days, I lay feeling absolutely wretched. With eyes closed when the door opens and one of my ex-roommates enters to enquire about my condition and the disposition regarding the doctor. I tell him of the last casualty and he informs me.

"I hear, no more men will be brought here to die by starving." He soon cheers me up with all the latest rumors. He leaves when I tell him of the promise of discharge the next day with certain conditions. Upon hearing this news he agrees to return tomorrow.

The next morning the bluff works with barely a look at me. This seems to be the doctor's routine more than an interest in a patient's well-being, but it gives me what I want, the discharge. Now the problem was how to get dressed? The same underwear was still on me that is part of the dressing process. While reaching for my pants that are on the foot of the bed, the door opens. In march my two conspirators. I am instantly chuffed to see their cheeky faces.

"Stand to, Shorty."

They dress me, hurrying to ensure my being on time. One carries me downstairs pick-a-back, seating me in the waiting-room to wait for the ambulance to take us to the convalescent centre. When it arrives the driver is not surprised at my being carried. He was told beforehand of my condition and that of others that prevailed in that "Valley of Hope."

From this moment on there is no other way to go but up. Because having survived that ordeal, due to the ingenuity of my mates, recovery is bound to come. A man is given the benefit of the doubt if he reports sick because of the unknown nature of this plague. Evidently he is given the same benefit on reporting back. That is only fair.

Forty-eight hours was the time allowance for convalescence. Then it was discharge for duty or report to this ship's sickbay. However, as there were no names taken of the men in this department, the doctor was not interested in keeping to the regulation, provided no one reported feeling worse when he called on us. Seeing this opportunity to stay without being noticed, I stayed one week until recovery. My recovery came, by having food that could be eaten along with some delicacies that were sent aboard each day by a thoughtful women's organization created to help the "flu victims."

It is now the first week in November. The news from the front is encouraging to the point where the end seems near and I have two days ashore to wait for my ship. At the end of that time she came in without the Commander and the good-luck Bunting-Tosser. While I was away the Old Man caught the flu. He was very sick and put aboard the Hospital Ship. Bunting-Tosser had passed the examination for a Mate's Certificate while on his leave and was given command of a minesweeper. His leaving had been the cause of many discussions and fears for his taking the whole of the halo served upon him by a Guardian Angel. During the time he was with us he taught me how to semaphore, as he was the only one doing this work. In doing so, he had a relief.

A boy from a training-ship, which was a reformatory school, was his replacement. With my having been ashore so much, I offered to relieve this lad. Being a weekend, he requested that much leave, which was granted because I was qualified.

At three o'clock Sunday, November 10, 1918, a general signal was sent to all ships in the harbour, "Stand By," for an important announcement. After a wait of fourteen hours it came, stating that an Armistice had been signed to become effective at eleven hundred hours. But that did not sink into the brain of the one in charge because he did not know the meaning of the word. Instead, he did his usual by slipping the moorings, heading out to sea. On approaching the entrance to the harbour, the man standing on the pier bellows through his megaphone.

"This war is over. Are you looking for another one?" He rapidly shouts, "No ships are permitted to leave," and "do not proceed."

So, what does my Skipper do? He drops anchor just inside the breakwater instead of getting back to the buoy that had been the Fletcher's property for more than four years.

At precisely eleven o'clock sirens start to blow, signifying the end of hostilities. Then all hell seems to let loose. Every vessel in the harbour that had been commandeered for the war has its guns pointed towards France and fires all the ammunition aboard. When it is all over, the guns are left uncovered and uncleaned. From this moment on no orders are given. Nothing is done but to eat, sleep, play cards and read mail.

Two days later the Cook receives a letter from the deckhand who had been his assistant until the time two and a half years before, when he put on his act of being driven-insane by Mary Ellen. He explains in detail about how he was under observation for four months before receiving his discharge and since that time he is receiving a small pension for his "acting disability."

He was more fortunate than one man who had reported that he had gone deaf to a point that he could hear absolutely nothing. He had persevered until the time came for his case to receive a final reviewing before a panel of doctors. They openly discussed his condition in his presence. He played his part so well, it was agreed that he should be discharged, so he was. He was much elated by the decision rendered but did not show it until he went through the door. On his way out a voice called out, "Close the door, please." He turned round and was grabbed immediately by a Crusher who rushed him to the Brig for ninety days.

He remembered later that he had closed the door. Now he was in a place where this plot could not be re-enacted.

For a whole month we lay at anchor. It was a long rowing distance for the two men who went daily to the Naval Pier for the mail. But because the loud (imaginary) voice had told the Skipper not to proceed farther into the harbour, he obeyed. The swearing grew louder with each passing day by the boat's crew. Had the men refused to go for the mail nothing in the way of punishment could have been imposed. They knew the mail was the only medium through which the next orders would come. The order came that we were to go into the dock, not for repairs or overhaul but just for the general public to view. Little did they know that this one hundred fifty-foot long vessel, the H.M.S. James Fletcher, has been the biggest ship on the Dover Patrol, for over four years?

A short distance from where we were tied up was a ketch with a small, scruffy-looking crew between us and the quay and a U254 German submarine, that was being brought in under its own power by a British Navy crew. It had been handed over as part of the Armistice agreement. During the berthing of the sub I hear a crewman reply to his Lieutenant Commander that is considered the height of disgusting insubordination. He was walking very slowly with the bow-line to put on the bollard on shore, when he is ordered to speed it up. Stopping in his tracks, turning, looking at his Commander, he replies.

"Look 'ere, Guvner, your old woman waited nine months for you, now you can wait a couple of bleedin' minutes for me."

It brought no reply other than a look of contempt from his superior, who if given the opportunity, looked as if he could knock the daylights out of him. Instead it brought a reply from the one who had stood by me when I was called a Jonah.

. He cooly says, "In a fair fight, if that is what you want, I will put my money on the Commander since you are taking advantage of his position, knowing that he is not allowed to fight."

Hearing this, the mouthy one calls my champion an "illegitimate" in the vulgar way. Anyone from Lancashire is sensitive to being called that. So he puts it upon himself to take the Commander's place and steps onto the quay to meet his adversary who is taller and about twelve years younger.

The Commander comments on it being a mismatch but is advised to wait and see. The younger man starts punching away. Every blow hitting the other below the head, as if that is the only part where he is vulnerable and is kept covered. Our man does not take the initiative for about the first three minutes. Then when he feels the blows becoming weaker he opens up, not with any amount of speed but with accuracy to the mouth while telling his opponent at the same time that he should never call a Lancashire lad what he did. When the mouthy one had been hit enough to extract an apology that is requested to end the affair, the Commander comes aboard to thank our man for substituting for him, also, to see for himself if he is hurt in any way. He strips to convince the Commander of his having felt no effects of the scrap and no sign of any. The Commander is awe-struck by what he sees. My friend exhibits a short stocky frame with numerous small muscles standing out like knots that seem just as hard. This accounts for letting his opponent hit him in the body until his hands get tired.

"You amaze me," the Commander shakes his head in disbelief, looking to me.

I grin. "Commander, Sir, for two and a half years it has been a requisite for this man to stop me daily from going along the deck until I spar flat-handedly for five minutes-punching him in the stomach to his satisfaction, before allowing me to proceed along the deck."

"I see where you reaped some benefit," he remarks.

"Yes Sir, I do." The muscles in my arms spoke for themselves.

The Commander sufficiently expressed his gratitude again before departing, with a, "Ta, ta ta," which we returned.

People came daily to the quay to see the inside of the submarine. Mostly women came because it was open during working hours. One man was stationed on deck to assist them down. Another man was at the bottom of the vertical ladder to prevent one from falling. In more ways than one it would have been most convenient had a staircase been installed but room did not permit it. Needless to say, the ladies' helpers performed their services most willingly.

The next attraction was the ketch with the unkempt crew. Outwardly it bore a resemblance to its crew but at short intervals the sides of the house on deck would collapse, revealing a four point-two with the gun's crew at respective positions, ready for action.

As for the James Fletcher, it has no attraction except for one male visitor who comes aboard into the forecastle, whereupon he spends the time in card games. He calls my name. I turn to see who it is, as the voice is unfamiliar. He is not in uniform. My first thought is that he is sent to take me to finish my sentence in the Union until I reach the age of twenty-one, now that the war is finished. I do not answer for this reason. In fact, no one replies for me although none know my reason.

After a moment of silence he says, "I don't know who this Fred is. No last name was given me but I just want to thank him for supplying me with cigarettes for two years while I was a prisoner of war in Germany."

Relieved that the Union did not send him but three of my crewmates are casting glances directly at me, I come forward. "That would be me." We shake hands.

His name was given to me by one to whom I had become attached. She told me she had a brother in a Lancer Regiment who had been captured very early in the war and that he would appreciate a letter from someone to help relieve the monotony. Navy men were able to buy cigarettes duty-free, if bought in bulk by the ship's company. However, at the same time, provided the money and address were furnished, an order would be sent to the one interned. Henceforth, at intervals of three months, the order was renewed that kept him well supplied, with some to spare for others. He came this day to show his gratitude. Even if he had not done so, it would not be upsetting. Knowing that the opportunity afforded itself in my having had experience with incarceration, I was able to partially relieve the misery of one with the same condition. Now that we had met there was no reason to stay aboard. So off to a pub we went to drink and talk about events of the war and the reason he did not get a letter from his mother during that time.

He was the oldest of four. Made fatherless through his father's death at an early age, he had always been treated as the black-sheep of the family for an unexplained reason. Before he was eighteen he joined the army, having served nine years until the time of his capture. He had two sisters and one brother who was given the opportunity to get a degree in dentistry and who at the time of being called up was given the rank of Second Lieutenant.

This created a problem by the fact that eating in the officers' mess room brought on an added expense. The Turkish or Egyptian cigarettes offered at the end of meals were costly, so he came to me requesting a supply of them—naturally with the promise and expectation of paying for them. The order on my part was filled. For that, he was very pleased. So much so, that he gave me a promise but never the payment. The popular saying among lower-deck ratings, although not always true, is, "One can't be an officer and a gentleman." It certainly was the case in this instance of two brothers. They both were mislabeled.

Following a month of loafing while in dock, the order came that we were all to go to the Paymaster's Office to fill out papers preparatory for discharge after the ship was handed back to its owner. The center of the room was taken up with tables pushed together to form a fairly large rectangle. Seated were a number of young women in the uniform of the Woman's Royal Naval Service, Wrens for short. They filled out the forms while behind them, each man had to stand to give the answer to the question asked in a quiet manner, so as not to confuse the next person. The first question asked of me standing behind a very pretty Wren, in a voice not much above a whisper, "What is your home address?"

"None," I answered.

Then without hesitation the pretty little spitfire opened up her mouth so that all could hear, requesting the "Crusher" to throw me out for not giving an answer to suit her. The Crusher by the way, is a Chief Petty Officer, standing about six feet tall, weighing around two hundred thirty pounds and is a member of the Naval Police.

He came to lay a hand on me when his attention was drawn to the man who substituted for the submarine commander, who called from the other side of the room telling me to use his home address.

The Crusher, turning to him said, "Why? Do you want the kid's money?"

The reply to that was, "Young fellow, don't say things to me like that unless you are sure you have something to back it up and don't lay a hand on that lad."

By this time the entire crew was standing by, trying to explain the circumstances to the Crusher who did not seem to grasp the situation. On the advise of my champion I left the room, passing the little spitfire who now had an apologetic look and a tear in her eye. I had caused the proceedings to stop. The girls were passing the word along about what had brought about this upheaval. As I was on the verge of leaving, the Crusher was being told that in over two years I had not been granted leave for the same reason. No home.

Later in the day I was informed that the Crusher conceded there was no other way to settle the dispute concerning me. My identification and protection certificate was completed without my presence; not by the pretty spitfire because her emotions got the upper-hand and she was left to cry. It appeared from the talk of the crew to the officers that quite a discussion was held trying to convince the Crusher that I had joined up with a doubtful name, no address or next of kin. Another matter that he could not understand was how anyone could join and serve three months without being signed up. After listening to all this the Crusher had drawn the conclusion, if during that time had anything fatal happened to me I would not have been missed by a soul. I had joined up without signing on and I was now being discharged the same way, as ridiculous as it may sound. It was true. But I wondered what information my mates had conjured for these documents? That wrote finis to the service in the Drifter Patrol of the Dover Patrol.

When the suggestion was put to me that with my not having a home, I would do well to stay in the Royal Navy. From a security point of view this was good advice, but the memories of the events of the past two and a half years had tainted me; such as, the Cossack trying to run through a concrete breakwater to get into the harbour; the wholesale massacre on the Vindictive; and the torpedoing of the Gorgan. These reminders made me to heed one other bit of advice given to me. Self-preservation was the first law of nature.

Two days later orders were received to proceed to Portsmouth for the dismantling of the guns and the unloading of the ammunition. The latter part of said order had been fulfilled on Armistice Day. Had it been at all possible, the guns would have gone with it. As of that day they had not even been cleaned or covered and now it was three months later. The motto bestowed on the Boy Scouts by their organizer, General Baden Powell, "Be prepared," had not been complied with for a number of possible reasons. Not caring or never having been in the movement, to train kids to sleep beneath the stars, might be two of the reasons. "Being prepared" was presumed to be a must in wartime, as no two wars have been fought alike, either on land or sea.

The dismantling was done at this renowned base. Next came an inspection for the extent of damage in order to recondition the ship and to reimburse the owners for the estimated cost in changing over to her original condition. After two days, the Paying-Off Tennant was hoisted onto the mainmast to go to the home-port of the James Fletcher, without her prefix, H.M.S. On arriving there it was near midnight. There was nothing more to do than wait for the morning when each man would be given his discharge, pay voucher and a free pass on the railroad to his home town. Instead, the Skipper mailed all these documents back to the Admiralty, leaving many hands stranded aboard. The amount of food allotted by the Navy was for three days. Two days' food had been used getting here.

One man could not contain himself at this turn of events. He called the Skipper everything that could only be printed in a special seaman's dictionary yet he hit the nail on the head when he said it had deliberately been done so that the Skipper would get the pay of a Lieutenant that was more than he could get from the owner in peace-time. Here we were without lights, water and food, while workmen were making inspections from the Navy list of defects given to them. On the third day word was received that we were to return to Portsmouth by train, to go through once more what had been done in Dover; to be re-discharged.

I went below in the dark to get my kit, confident that I would find it. But I literally fell just short of getting it because an inspector had left the hatch open to inspect the bilges. So down I went, not to such a depth but enough to hurt both my back and head and I was unable to move at least for a while. Then realizing that there was no one around to help me I clambered out, dragging myself to the chart room to lie on the padded-lockers. When trying to pull myself up, the cushion came off, then putting my finger through the hole in the lid, that came away, revealing twenty-four Webley Colt pistols, that none of the crew knew existed. The Navy men had overlooked them and now these men had not seen them. There was no one to whom I could report this without delaying the trip for discharge. So I waited until I boarded the train to write a letter to the champion of mine who was left behind to act as the night-watchman until the final acceptance of the ship by her owners. That letter was mailed at the first stop on the journey to Portsmouth. He would give it to the proper Navy man.

Arriving there somewhat tired, dirty and still very sore from the fall, I was obliged to cross the parade grounds to apply for bedding. Being late afternoon the area was deserted with the exception of one blue-jacket in gaiters, belt and a whistle dangling from his neck.

Seeing me walking he blew the whistle loudly then ordered me to go "on the double." When he saw that I did not obey the command he hurried toward me with a loud reprimand but when I told him of the discomfort that I was suffering, that I had to get the hammock before the supply room closed, then I would report to the sickbay. He gave me to understand that at all times a lower-deck rating, regardless of the hour of the day, had to cross the grounds on the double. The only ones excused are those with a chit from the doctor that had to be carried in the hand for the guard to see. When he saw I was in pain, he reached into his pocket, extracting a plain piece of paper and gave it to me.

"Carry this chit, you poor bastard. Why didn't you wait a couple of days longer to fall in the 'ole because these restrictions will be lifted then?"

From a Navy man one can expect to hear humour before sympathy, regardless of its being insulting yet at the same time not being offensive.

Pompey Barracks was the only Naval place with these restrictions, that had been imposed exactly ten years before when the men refused to obey the command of an officer. This necessitated calling the marines out to quell the mutiny that ensued. There was enough class distinction shown on railway coaches such as first, second and third. But when one person has the unmitigated gall to order hundreds of men to degrade themselves in the manner he requested, what alternative did they have but to show resentment?

Could this, then, be the reason why the saying is so popular, "One can't be an officer and a gentleman," when one of their kind issues the command, "On your knees you dogs"? To my knowledge there were no casualties, but rest assured, had that officer been within reach, he could have put in a request for roses.

Two days after the ten-year penalty on the barracks had been lifted, I got my discharge with a month's pay and thirty days leave amounting in time to three years thirteen days. With these precious gifts was a railway pass to the only address that was partially mine.

Oh, to go anywhere far away from the grim reminders of the horrors of the Dover Patrol and the Union. I was free at last from institutional supervision after fifteen years. But I was lonely with my personal feelings. It was this way because when meeting people, as a stranger in any town, would prompt their asking, "Where is your home?" Upon reaching my destination I lost no time in looking for a berth on a ship that would take me and keep me far away. But no such luck came my way.

8

Frenchy Becomes Fisherman

The only industry in the town where I had an address was trawler fishing. This method of fishing calls for a large conical shaped net that is dragged along the sea's bottom, but not necessarily having colours such as red, blue, green or brown. Trawling was being done by half-deck boats for prawns; by smacks with beam-trawls and by steam trawlers that ranged from crabbers that did not catch crabs. They were classified as such because they were smaller and fished not far from home. The larger ones went distances ranging from three hundred miles south of Ireland to the Faroe Islands, Iceland and places in between.

The first two types of fishing were done to fill in for those who stay year in and year out in the same craft. This was generally termed "Ignorant fishermen" who made up the crew of the "Hell Wagons," sometimes referred to as steam trawlers. To my amazement, finding out how scientific these trawls are designed surely belied the stigma attached to the men who worked them. Regarding their being ignorant is not true.

The requirements to obtain a mate's license for trawling was to have at least four years at sea, with two of those years serving at deep-sea fishing. As soon as I had put in that amount of time I went for my mate's license and got it on first try, but the opportunity to use it did not come until nearly three years later when I accepted an opening on a trawler. If "Lady Brittania" ruled the waves she did a poor job of controlling one little fledgling, a crabber. Due to her behavior she was called every nautical name that was most impolite, even to the point of being unlawful to be used in public. In order to show a little discretion in this case, she shall be in a distinctive category, as "Hell Wagon de Luxe."

The name may imply this crabber as being a vehicle. Instead, it is centered on a steam trawler that sailed sometimes from the third largest fishing port in the British Isles at the time. The name is sometimes used with awe and reverence in connection with the S.T. Cevic, the queen of them all. She had gone to far away places such as those that the larger trawlers went to but that was during the war.

Since that time she had acquired some habits. One habit being that she absolutely refused to be nursed in stormy weather. I spent the last three months of her oceanic career aboard her, not only as a mate but as a detective also, trying to solve her mysterious behavior. She would go under at the first ripple on the water and not clear her deck until this tub was under the lee of Great Ormes Head or the Isle of Man.

The reward for giving loyal service for five years to one owner of trawlers in the capacities of deckhand and boatswain was to be honoured with a title of second in command to the "Bitch of the Sea." The question may arise that if she was so misbehaved, what in the hell was the reason for not quitting after the first trip, instead of staying for eleven more successive trips? The first part of the question can readily be answered by stating that she was moored in the dock near an unused grain elevator. This building is mentioned here because it played a part in the life of our heroine. Her history had been kept a secret and I was ignorant regarding her habits. The second part of the question can be answered with one word-stupidity, but not without reservation. At least it gave me the chance to get time in toward the one year required as mate before taking the examination to be a skipper.

So I go aboard and put to sea to fish in home-waters. All is well, weather-wise, for the first week. Then a slight breeze springs up that causes the boatswain to tell the Skipper to "run for shelter." With my knowing the boatswain very well I refrain from making any comment but the Old Man just laughs it off. Shortly thereafter he heeds the warning because the wind freshens slightly. We heave the trawl and set about catching the fish that we had previously caught because the deck crew is now knee-deep in water.

As mentioned before, I know the boatswain very well. The first time I met him he was in the same capacity in another hell-wagon while I was a deckhand and his watch-mate. This meant that we were to share the wheel, steaming to and from the fishing grounds. That generally took from one to five days for vessels other than crabbers. The day was divided into four six-hour watches with only two men in each watch doing two of these watches daily.

No license was required to be boatswain, yet this man cannot be anything more because he has very poor eyesight. A discovery I had made earlier on our first night-watch together. When he was standing in front of the wheel his eyes were close to the overhead compass and we were two points off course. From that moment on I was to become the best watch-mate he ever had because I took the wheel for five and a quarter hours out of the six. He is known as Harry, a tall lean man of about sixty and the only one I ever saw who works with bare arms from the shoulders the whole year through.

There are many deep-sea fishermen who are allergic to salt water. Boils on their arms are attributed to the sleeves chaffing them. Some get them in large numbers and some in clusters of small boils while others get the huge variety. The number would vary from thereabouts forty of the small kind. One man had twenty-six of the large boils just on his forearms that looked painfully inflamed. There was no treatment for boils nor did it excuse one from working.

Harry is the only man I know who would get boils above his elbows and could not prevent their coming at the risk of getting something worse. Now Harry and I are in this career-thing together. The time has come when he can only get what nobody else wants regarding his line of work, such as these lousy ships. We both agree that this is the worse ship to handle.

It is now time to eat. Those present at the table are complaining about the ship except the second engineer who expresses an optimistic point of view by stating that no one could hold his job without fear of another taking it. Of course your life was not worth much while serving on this Hell Wagon but there is some sense in what he says because it is a privilege in this firm for the skipper to bring the mate of his choosing, usually a relative. In this regard there is not a remote chance for me to be this skipper's mate. I now know that my job I have is secure for what it is worth.

This vessel has another problem contributed by the unused grain elevator, where she has been tied up for so long. In the cabin floor are a number of holes about two inches in diameter. Holes are also in the bottom of the four bunks above the transom lockers. These lockers are used for storing lentils and periodically there would emanate from them a sound resembling a scream.

We put into a small town in the north of Wales and tie up astern of another crabber of the same company. The mate of her is a friend of mine. I happen to be alone in the cabin when he comes aboard to see me and the rest of the crew goes visiting on his ship. While he is in a leaning position against the end of the table and talking to me, the scream comes from the opposing factions from within the lockers. He immediately freezes, his face white with fright. He is speechless for about a minute then turns to me.

"What was that?"

I reply, "Rats."

Upon his leaving I am left alone to muse as to the best way I could get along with these creatures. With their being around it gives me another sense of security in the fact that while they are aboard, this ship would at least stay in the vicinity of the surface.

How many of them crawled over me will never be known. A man could sit on the lockers and watch the little rascals crawl over the engineers and the cook, not even respecting the authority of the skipper who was not exempt. I counted as many as five on the second engineer at one time. My bunk was in the same cabin. It is doubtful that there was anything on me to deter them. It became clear to me that it was my responsibility, sitting there alone to ponder, as to the best method of ridding this sweetheart of a ship of these pests and also to solve the mystery as to what makes her a partial submarine?

Provisions such as potatoes and fresh vegetables on steam-trawlers are generally kept in the lifeboat but in this case tradition is broken. The boat is cleared of produce and we make it a practice to inspect it. Along with gripes and bellyaches we also inspect the slip hook, turnbuckles and chains that keep it in place following each haul of the trawl, in order to be ready at all times for launching. Next comes the inspection of the bilges with hand-pumps. It produces nothing as to the cause for submarine behavior.

This ship has become a mystery ship. Only a few years before she had been used to fish off the coast of Iceland at the time when all the larger trawlers had been commandeered by the government for minesweeping. The former skipper is now retired after having made a fortune during the war in this Brittanic Product. He is now the owner of a fleet of his own yet he does not buy this bitch when she was lain up for so long. He is later put to the test when he opens his big fat mouth regarding the ability of her.

The first trip ends. The skipper and the crew leave her, with the exception of the second engineer, to whom I will refer to in the future as Second, and myself. The exterminator is sent aboard. Needless to say he does a great job of bringing them back alive. He does enough to vindicate the owner by placing about a few small pieces of bread and butter with arsenic. This remains untouched throughout the next trip. I have eight tails to show for my efforts. That amounts to one for each trap that I set. After each catch in a trap, I keep sterilizing the trap to catch another; boiling, steaming and smoking, but to no avail. If the volume of the screams is reduced because of their numbers being reduced by eight, it is not in the least noticeable. These traps were all given to us by passing trawlers at sea who were contacted by semaphore. Was the reason for not catching more might be due to the fact that the rats knew that they did not belong on the Cevic?

On one occasion I set a trap on the pantry floor. I close the door and by the time I reach a locker about six feet away to sit, it goes off. By the time I reach the trap the animal has its tail bitten in three places where the gang is trying to rescue him. At this end of the small-game hunt I now know how many of them are left. Answer: X-8, providing the pregnant ones do not give birth as of this second. The war between the rival factions goes on daily and fortunately no member of the crew is ever bitten.

Our second Skipper is one who has never been on a steam trawler but has spent forty-seven years on smacks. On the way down the channel, outward bound, he expresses his philosophy to me.

"I've done well in sailing trawlers and see no reason for not doing better in steam ships." He brought his younger son on as the boatswain who had a skipper's license for steam trawlers, just to give him pointers on hauling and shooting the trawl. Three days later he found to his dismay that he could not do better in steam than sail. At least, not in this instance because a breeze sprang up, although not a hard blow but enough to scare the hell out of him and the crew. Needless to say, he took her back home when the opportunity came, with a vow that this was his last trip in a steam trawler.

Number three Skipper is the older son of the previous one. Except for Second and me, there is a complete change of crew. He (Second) and I, once at sea on this trip, assume ownership of this craft. He is to have that part that is below deck and my portion is everything from the deck to truck, meaning those things on the topmasts that halyards are rove. Supported also by Second, each trip starts by an argument with the cook to keep the lifeboat clear of produce.

The new Skipper was made to go on this trip much against his will. It was a case of, "Take her or else." His name is Jim and he is crippled with a split thigh. At the time of the accident he was a boatswain but had a skipper's license. A pin broke in the after-gallast sheave. It weighed about one hundred pounds and was accompanied by the otter board with a weighted shoe of fifteen hundred pounds, that all came down on his left thigh. He was taken to a port in the south of Ireland and then by car to a hospital in Cork where he was confined for eighteen months. There was no insurance coverage of any kind available to the deep-sea fishermen, due to the dangers encountered. Now this is where the, "or else," takes place.

When Jim was able to get around with a limp that would be his for all his life, the owner of the Hell Wagon de Luxe gave him a job of unloading ships in the docks, by way of compensation. The workday began at five in the morning, six days of the week. He stayed on this job until no skipper could be found for this "bastard" on which Second and I were having so much fun. By first encounter, the crewmates are in agreement with the opinion of the Skipper. One of the deckhands expresses our feelings to him in no uncertain terms.

"Skipper, me and my mates want to make things clear to you befor' we get under way. We don't want your help to haul the trawl an' we don't want to see you on deck, unless it's for your personal reasons. Are you comfy with this?"

Jim's surprised face turned into a hearty grin. "Aye, sir, no need for flags, I get the message."

We, the two owners while at sea, make plans to see that this trip would be curtailed as soon as possible without jeopardizing the Skipper's future, such as it is. Jim enjoyed dancing-his way of doing pleasurable exercise by attending the local hop every Friday night.

We cast off early on a Tuesday. The weather is fine and we keep a constant watch on the Skipper, as this is his first trip since meeting with his accident. It is a pitiful sight to see him trying to keep his footing on the steel deckhouse to go to the bridge. Having seen enough of this for three days out the plan that Second suggests is put to the boatswain, for him to persuade the deckhands to refuse to work for the Skipper who is not safe. Forced persuasion is not needed to influence them to execute the plan that includes the rats. In fact, they are intending to sever all relations with the Cevic and rats in a mutinous manner, had not this convenient suggestion been put to them. Their expressions are not so delicately worded but their support is to be relied upon. They are not in the least reluctant to leave this "arrogant lady" with her brood to Second and me, stating that we are a pair of bloody fools to stay with her. At least we have our jobs with no fear of losing them, although it is not paying me anything because I am on commission of the net earnings, whereas Second is on a stipulated amount.

Jim has no alternative but to take her back. On arriving he gets the support of the firemen and cook, who profess they took his meals to the bridge, the liars. The Skipper is back in good time for the dance this night. He also gets his job back without fear of being pushed around again. He is one of the nicest fellows to know. This brings us to the end of the third trip. Still my partner remains silent about leaving this "Ruby of the Ripples," so I stay just as stupid and do likewise, as each one of us is waiting for the other to break.

By this time it is known throughout the town that the thing I am trying to do is to make a fortune from submerged treasure, without success, of course. This vessel is the only one that does not have spuds in the lifeboat. In order to avoid arguments with the cook, instructions are given to the deliverymen to that no fresh produce is to be stored in the lifeboat.

Now it is time to venture on the fourth trip, with as usual a complete new crew with the exception of two idiots; the following quote still holding true that, "To know naught is to fear naught." About this time the tragic news comes that a trawler had run on the shoals off the Isle of Man with all hands lost. She had left home late that afternoon in foul weather. Harry was the boatswain; in all probability he had the watch, as it was the usual procedure for the mate to take the wheel in the channel; then for the boatswain to take over afterwards. So, most likely that was the case. Another usual procedure was that before going to sea the pubs did quite a bit of business with the crews in the way of repairing thirsts. The whole town knew how bad Harry's sight was but the ship's husband whose duty it was to furnish crews for the ships did not care who was signed on, provided he could move.

It was the average to lose a ship with all hands each winter. That was the gamble of the job; to risk lives and get nothing while one had it or get absolutely nothing when it was lost. Knowing this yet I continue to be one of the biggest idiots in the town. But what else does this idiot know? I thought of changing careers ofttimes but to what and where would I live in the meanwhile? The question was never asked of me, "Did you have a good catch this trip?" Instead, it was put this way. "Did you catch anything this trip?" When it was asked I came to the conclusion that people can be rude at times although the nail was still hit on the right head.

The new Skipper is a young man of twenty-three. The rest of the crew is younger, thereby giving me seniority in age and service on this "Associate of Mermaids." It is appropriate to mention a minor detail, that as we are on our way out through the lock-gates, the Dock Master's voice rings out loud and clear.

He shouts on seeing us, "Who in the hell let school out?"

There may have been something appropriate in that remark. For the record it can be said that all of our rear-ends were nearer the deck than our heads were to basket-ball hoops. A lad's future counts more on work survival than on other activities in this country.

Trip number four lasts nine days with fine weather all the way. Our "Dead Girl" creates no problems other than sheltering the many passengers with tails that scare the crew, with the exception of one. His name is Johnny. We had been shipmates before, with rats, too. He is the only bare handed man rat-catcher that I have ever seen. Johnny is five feet one-inch in height. He would lunge for a rat, catch it, turn to me and tell me to watch its eyes turn white as he puts a squeeze on each side of the neck with his thumb and finger. Until this time I have been afraid of these devils but never do I attempt to do what he has shown me. But later I do a trick that he has shown me when one gets into the flour-bin. He tells me to flick some flour into its eyes then pick it up.

The reason for this being so easy to do is that rats cannot close their eyes and the flour quickly forms a paste. More could be said about Johnny and his animal-hunts but it is not a pleasant subject to relate. Needless to say this rat condition does not improve.

At the end of trip number four there is one less replacement when the Old Man is taking out the "Bitch on Brine" for another go and so here we have the first repeater. When he makes this announcement to me, Second is informed and answers by saying that it is his (the Old Man's) prerogative but the Old Man will not have a share in our ship. Actually a skipper is the owner of a ship while at sea. To prove this point, I have been a watch-mate of a mate who has been skipper of a trawler that he next sold for five hundred pounds. The new owners made one trip before it was reclaimed but they were able to make a nice profit on their investment.

On trip number five it is a most unusual sight to see the same Skipper. The rest of the crew is new with the exception of the two fixtures. No comment is made this time by the Dock Master in passing through the locks, as this deck-crew is more advanced in years, also in ignorance by coming on this wagon.

During the first meal at sea the Old Man breaks the news to me. "Shorty, I told the office I'll be replacing you for another mate when we get back. He'll be waiting when we come ashore."

My answer comes readily without quivering, hesitation or malice afore-thought, "Skipper, you will not be here next trip."

Support came immediately from Second who said in like manner, "You are so right, Shorty."

Both of these remarks went without comment, that left the Skipper quiet for the next couple of days. He knew there was no sign of mutiny but he must have wondered why I answered him with so much confidence.

I was playing the law of averages because we had nine days of fair weather on the previous trip; one fine day at home; followed by two more days of fine weather. I knew it had to break soon. The weather breaks on the third day out with all the signs of a storm. A slight breeze springs up and it is left to me to tell the Skipper to seek shelter but he just laughs. Once again we set about catching the fish that had been caught and to keep ourselves above water, despite the warning. The trawl is hauled and the ends pulled in so that we could run for shel-ter under the lee of the East coast of Ireland as the wind is from the northwest.

After a bad time at sea the Old Man breaks his silence by giving vent to his feelings against this "Sister of a Submarine." From this moment on Second and I are welcome to her. What the owner should do with her is not a fitting matter to print and too delicate a subject to discuss for my sensitive ears that have been to sea for only eight years. We end in the sheltered waters until the weather improves then leave for home, with renewed security that my job is not in jeopardy. The minute we step ashore the Skipper invites Second and me to join him in some elbow-bending exercises in the Royal Oak. Eventually as friends we part, with a, "Ta, ta ta," to us. But to the girl he left behind, tied up in dock, his parting remark was far from pleasant.

At the end of each curtailed trip standing on the dock upon the arrival of the Cevic, would be her wartime skipper, who made a fortune in her. He made an imposing picture as he stood with hands in pockets and a gold chain stretched across a huge gut that was growing as fast as the chasm just beneath his nose. His talk reached the point where, according to him, there was never a better fishing vessel built. He was entitled to that opinion but it was a different matter to stand with two cronies and ridicule our Skipper. I was hoping that I would be around to see that big fat mouth closed, regarding the ability and disposition of our "Heroine."

Her owner now found a way to get her skipper and crew for this "Cradle of the Deeper Deep." He had over seventy trawlers, so there was always at least one out of service for overhaul. The skipper of such a trawler, instead of waiting for the work to be completed would be asked to take the "Precious One" for a trip. This seemed a reasonable suggestion but it was near Christmas and this man who was assigned to take her out was looking forward to being home for the holidays. Ship owners do not want their vessels to be in port on holidays or weekends because of dock dues. That was the main reason for keeping the Cevic going. She was not catching enough fish to show a profit but it was less expensive to go to sea. One thing was certain she had not made any money for me. The only thing of benefit by my staying was getting the time in towards becoming a skipper but I was doing it at the risk of losing life or limb, as so many had done but still that did not make sense.

This Skipper, number five on trip six, decided to take "Honey" a little farther than his predecessors by going to fish off the South Wales coast, not Australia, God forbid! It is essential to mention this because one chief engineer who had risked losing everything for one trip aboard this "Glorious Girl" was one of the crew that took a steam trawler from Fleetwood, England to Vancouver, British Columbia. That was before the Panama Canal was opened to take a trawler no larger than the Cevic round the Horn, which was no mean feat. In all probability our "Heroine" would have made that trip in her younger days but now old age had crept over her, making her too feeble to rise over a ripple on the water.

After two days of fishing "Dear One" developed internal trouble. The furnace crowns were coming down. This meant the boiler would have to be blown down. Luckily Fishguard was reached safely. This was a small port that was the terminal for the Great Western Railway, from which passengers caught the boat to Dublin. It was the year that Ireland was made a Free State. The station was crowded with men in Navy uniforms who had accepted their discharges to show their loyalty to the new nation. The majority of them had imbibed too freely to celebrate that event and the Christmas Holidays. When I entered the pub in the town I was asked by the publican to assist one man, who had drunk too much, to the quay to get the boat. For reasons of personal safety it was necessary to talk with a brogue, as this crowd was ugly.

The repairs to the boiler took nine days because the work was being done by one man who had to ply between ship and shore by small boat. The Skipper knowing about this inconvenience gave orders to remove the fish from the hold to prevent its going bad. The hotel in town had plenty of fish and I got the only money that I ever made in this "Fortune-Maker." Second wanted no part of the money because as he put it, that was in the part of the Cevic that I owned. So to even matters, the boiler-repairman dug into his pocket for Second that would go on the bill. It's an ill wind that blows no good.

Now we weigh anchor to resume our standard operational proceedings for the rest of the trip and with five more trips to follow. With the exception of the customary two there are the Skipper and crew and the regular greeting from Big Mouth who would always repeat the accomplishments of the great ship, Cevic.

While this is going on a small crowd starts gathering that gives the blabber-mouth encouragement to continue his tirade. When it reaches the point where it gets to be boring during a pause, a voice from the crowd says, "Show us or shut up." The crowd supports the heckler. A decision has to be made. This is the moment I have waited for; when someone would step aboard this "belligerent daughter of Father Neptune" with the ability to make a little bit of money. Then I could enter my hometown pubs, pay for my drinks and possibly treat some of the fellows who had helped me in support of my blotter-pad habit for the past three months.

Even though I thought I knew the "Cevic" there was no intent to draw conclusions about this to the eleventh Skipper for the twelfth trip. He said that he would take her on the next trip, to the satisfaction of the gathering. The group dispersed with words of praise and best wishes. He did not make any special request for personnel or material but accepted the new crew minus the two idiots who were now becoming a topic of beer drinking conversation.

Two days after this conference on the dock, the time had come for us to venture on a most memorable trip; one that has never duplicated by any trawler of this town. The weather is miserable-raining, with a strong southerly wind. Into this we head. Halfway down the buoyed channel our "Fortune-Maker" starts to put on her usual act but this time it has to be different because there is no room to turn round. Before getting under way the usual check-ups are made and the crew informed as to what to expect in the event of running into bad weather. The Skipper, realizing that this was a surprise, turns to me, shaking his head, and says, "This is not the same Cevic," but speaks no more. He is realizing now that he has spoken out of turn when he ridiculed the skippers who had been on this ship's bridge before him.

This is the moment I have waited for, not so much as to criticize, but to remind him that the safety of the crew comes first, that their lives should not be risked for the sake of being kidded. If he should turn her about at the end of the channel, then all would be well for their return. He is reminded that he has the most to lose. At this point the channel is nothing more than a breakwater but the lighthouse must be reached in order to turn her about. At least a lot of anxiety is removed in knowing that a lifeboat station is only a mile away with a capable crew of fishermen who would not take long in coming to our aid, if needed.

The Old Man knows this ship but Second and I know her, too. That makes us the best authorities of the pranks of this "Unintended-to-be Submarine." Second also knows that his part of the vessel would get protection. The thought of her going down all the way does not enter my head but I am mostly concerned about going into the engine room. In a number of ships of this design and age, the boiler is fired in the engine room therefore, should the fires go out here the "dear girl" would obstruct the channel for a while.

Eventually we turn about and get back in the dock on the same tide that we have left on. No one criticizes this man who on so many occasions had so much to say. Before going ashore he shakes hands with Second and me and with a parting remark says, "She should not be allowed out anymore." Later upon his recommendation to the legitimate owner she was tied up once again, alongside the grain elevator. The provisions were removed, otherwise within a few hours there would be none left.

During our ordeal it was consolation to know that the rats were still aboard, without venturing to leave. Had I known that they were not there when I came aboard at any time, the trip before would have been my last. We had been ship-mates long enough to know one another and I seemed to think they answered my call to them, but then again they could be heard at all times either scratching or jabbering among themselves. They could have been aboard for one reason, because they had consumed whatever grain could be found in their last home. Now when all was devoured on the Cevic there was no alternative for them but go to another trawler or trawlers. It seemed that little was done to reduce their numbers after hearing the hair-raising experiences of the night watchmen. Peri-odically, they had been seen leaving a trawler in formation, with their leader car-rying a straw in its mouth. Migrating rats are known to devour everything in their path that moves, so the watchmen had presence of mind to remain still on the approach of such an army. However, there was one trawler I had been on that had only one rat. It would come on deck at night while the crew was working, staying at a distance, bothering nobody. It was all white. It is said that with a white rat aboard, none of the grey ones will come aboard.

Now that I am beached, it was time for me to go to the office for a Bill of Set-tlement, in short, the payment of seven and one-half per cent of the net earnings of the "Fortune-Maker." In pretty red ink the total is written in beautiful hand-writing that I have further interest in the company because I now owe him twelve pounds. After questioning the validity of the statement in no uncertain terms, I am soon convinced of its veracity-when a man six feet four inches tall, weighing about two hundred twenty-five pounds informs me that it is correct. It is bound to be right when the questioner is less than five feet four inches and weighing but one hundred twenty pounds.

During this most friendly dispute the owner comes out and after being informed of the details, comes up with a wonderful suggestion in behalf of my welfare. He proposes my going with a skipper who is making money. In that way the debt would be paid. Is it not nice to know that in these conditions one could still work day and night in all kinds of weather for absolutely nothing, and risk the loss of limb or life while doing so? With my failing to give approval of this generous offer, he suspends me from getting a mate's job for three months. My parting answer is that he should make it for thirty years and on no account is the ship's husband to call me out of bed to go on a tide sail because a mate did not show.

At three o'clock the very next morning, there is a loud knocking on the door, the person is admitted and I am informed to get quickly ready as a trawler in need of a mate, has tied up outside the dock.. At first I refuse but then relent, due to the pleadings of the sweet soul who has asked me four years before to fill a spot in her home, with her husband and one son. She has had five sons but four had died, whose ages ranged from thirteen hours to twelve years. I have this place that is a home with love and understanding, to the point where at no time am I asked a question as to my past. There is the best of music and a church just across the street, which is a reminder to keep the home this way. The philosophy of this Lancashire Lass could not be ignored when she tells me, "This may be a good trip for you."

Can one expect to find this kind of outlook on life from one who has suffered such losses? She also started to work in cotton mills at the age of nine, caused by the death of her father. He was an employee, killed by a train when visiting a friend on his day off. That entitled the dependents to no insurance compensation.

A short walk with my sea kit and I am soon aboard. Losing no time in getting to the wheelhouse to meet the Skipper only to have my heart sink to my shoes at first sight of him. He is a man of unusual talent in this line of endeavor. He has established a record that has never been matched and he is appropriately nicknamed. Now that it is too late to turn back, I realize why the mate who was assigned for this job did not report. The Skipper is referred to as "Lockdoors." The term is used when a trawl is shot and it lands on the ocean-bottom fouled up by the two doors. Instead of spreading out the netting becomes closed. When this happens it is necessary to haul and shoot again, taking at least an hour of hard and dangerous work. This man has performed this act twenty-three times in one twelve-day trip. Two of the days were taken up steaming to and from the fishing grounds. Needless to say, there is no conversation between us.

The results of this trip show an increase in my debt and a little more time in towards becoming a skipper but that is now completely out of my mind because this very poor catch brings the most vulgar language from this devoted church-going owner.

He forgot that I am the same person he had told that he would put me with a money-making skipper only he was "putting in" his pocket in preference to mine. When he was told in front of a group to learn to talk like a man, I am suspended for all time. It so happens that the ship's-husband was one who heard it but before he had time to tell me to ignore it, it was made known to him that it will stick.

So ends my five years of life in "Hell Wagons" with investments in the firm that would never accrue dividends or to have me attend a stockholders' meeting. I am only to be thrown out by the lout-skipper who fought in the finals for the prospect of meeting Jack Johnson and winning the heavy weight crown. This elimination program was sponsored by an American, resulting in his taking back with him one who had the pseudonym, Horizontal, attached to him.

9

Trawling and Traveling

Since there was nothing else in this town for an unknown and unskilled worker to make a livelihood, if that was at all possible, then the alternative had to be reached. Dover was off my job-shopping list. I did not want to go back there. Too many painfully unhappy memories prevented my return. Lancaster did not want me due to the spread of the word of my being terminated. What could I do? Be a "Page" again or go back to the sea? New surroundings were needed.

Liverpool was in a serious post-war deprivation stage and also losing its shipping trade, yet that is where my first try is made to get a berth. When a ship needs a crew, men seeking jobs are required to go aboard. With the boatswain standing beside the chief officer, he would point to the men he wants. With my having followed the crowd just two days after being discharged therefore, still being in uniform, I was hoping to stand a better chance. Everybody else was dressed in mufti, with the exception of one soldier. The crew was chosen leaving only two who were not, the ones in uniform. We stood looking at each other a minute before we struck up an acquaintance. We decided to discuss matters over a brew; then parting, fully convinced that we had done a foolish act.

In the course of our suds-licking conversation my acquaintance tells me. "You know I hear it's easy to get a job on those tankers in Swansea."

"No, I did not know. Will you be heading off that way?"

"No, mate, not me. I saw enough fireworks in the war to last me a whole lifetime. No way will you get me on any tanker with her belly filled with boom-boom fluid."

I reached Swansea alone, as the soldier did not relish the idea of living so close to a volatile fluid. This Welch city could equally boast of affluence and penury The ships on the docks were practically begging for crews to do trips lasting but twenty-eight days while merchant-seamen sought jobs on vessels making long trips.

I was assigned to a ship that was fairly new and was carrying clean cargo to be unloaded in European ports before going for another load to take to a port in the United Kingdom, other than her port of registry. That trip took four months.

On the second trip an experiment was conducted with this tanker by loading her with aviation fuel. After twenty-four hours during which time a careful watch was kept on one hundred tons that were pumped into the Persian Gulf, due to that amount of its expansion.

After the third trip she was put on black oil to preserve the plates in the tanks. That meant short trips that did not have appeal for me to continue. Also, one's health can be greatly affected by danger with spending too much time in the oil regions of the Near East.

In this tanker port the Seaman's Union had no power to extort dues as they did in other shipping ports. This union when originally organized was expected to be for the benefit of the seamen, but this is a matter of conjecture, because its founder was a ship owner, also a Parliament member. One could not get a job unless his dues were paid up-to-date before being picked as one of a crew. The union did not have any say in securing employment for a person. There was no alternative because there was so much unemployment. Owing to my good record in my discharge book, a must in the rules of the union, I was able to get a berth on a nine thousand ton freighter. I made pleasant and interesting runs with her to a number of ports on the West Coast of America just before and during the prohibition era. This ship was built during this period and possibly for it. She was a six-hatch job with insulation in number two-hatch, for carrying bananas from the Panama Canal to San Pedro. Number one hold was loaded to the top with whiskey. The other four hatches had a little general cargo.

After being loaded with this prized beverage in Glasgow, the general cargo loaded in Manchester, then London; the next stop was Colon in the Panama Canal. There the Customs Officers would board her to put seals on the hatches of the contraband but they certainly did not know that all of that precious stuff could be removed without breaking the seals.

She was constructed in such a way that the bulkhead in the 'tween—deck separating numbers one and two holds, was not in line with the one beneath. It was about two feet forward of it. This was not noticeable when going down the ladder at the after-end of number two. That was a diversion, if not a violation, of the general rule of ship construction, but there is always somebody at sometime to discover this minute detail and the reason for it being so built.

This discovery was kept a secret by the one man who could find out things like this-to use to his advantage. He had only to report to the First Mate where he was working without supervision on any particular day. That man was the carpenter called Chips. This knowledge did not come to light until a year later, when Chips, after my third trip in her, was told not to sign on for the next trip.

After the rest of us had signed on for the fourth trip, two of us went to the pub nearest the shipping office. In there, enclosed in a cubicle, was a voice that was very familiar, narrating the secret as to how one could gain entrance into number one hold without breaking the seal of the Customs. In the forward-end of number two, tween-deck was a small insulated-hatch, kept shut by a padlocked grating. The nuts of the bolts had been loosened on the hasp of the lock, then greased and put back finger-tight. There was no danger of losing the nuts, if dropped, as they would land on the small hatch. Chips was not giving this information to any crewmember he was telling somebody how smart he was.

To prove his point and to put it to the test was a simple matter. As it turned out three cases containing twelve bottles each were discovered missing at the port of delivery, Vancouver, British Columbia. Up to this point everything seemed to be above-board as this cargo was unloaded on hand-trucks, and into the warehouse, then out the next door up the gang-way of the scruffiest looking craft imaginable. I found out later that she had a speed of twenty-two knots. This ship was keeping up with the times, along with three others that were plying the same route; one month apart. She had accommodations for sixteen passengers who were able to bathe in fresh water. Another modern feature was that there was a separate sleeping compartment where the sailors could keep their ration of one pail of water per day, instead of keeping it in the forecastle where men ate, provided it was fit food for human consumption.

That pail of water had to serve a three-fold purpose. At five in the afternoon the boatswain would take the padlock off the pump when the deck-crew was lined up to fill each pail. That water was used first for bathing, then the underwear and dungarees were washed, then for three meals a man washed his eating utensils. For hygienic purposes a cupful of water was extracted to brush teeth.

The disgusting food that was served did not in the slightest comply with the Board of Trade scale, because that had not been revised since the eighteen nineties. This then was the gratuity for answering the call of a few years earlier that proclaimed, "Your King and Country Need You."

It was most ridiculous to say that one was an ex-service man to any official because the prepared statement was always the same, "One of Millions." In 1909 when those seamen were called, "dogs," it may have been the only time nevertheless the treatment received was comparable to that time.

The main reason for being submissive was due to the fact that a man had a discharge-book for every trip and ship that was retained by the First Mate until the completion of a trip. With a bad discharge one could only get a job on ships in worse conditions. There were plenty of those ships still around looking for seamen. There were no bad discharges at the end of this trip for me because the Old Man did not find out who had taken the three cases of booze from the cargo although two hands had been caught selling the stuff later on in St. Johns, Oregon. Those two men went ashore with seventeen bottles to supply the proprietor of the little restaurant at the end of the quay. He had come around to the ship in the afternoon for the purpose of making contact with a provider and was told that he could have three-dozen bottles at five dollars each, payment in cash only. He agreed to stay after closing time and told them to come with the stuff at eight o'clock. The appointment was kept but he had only thirty-five dollars in cash, offering to pay the balance with a cheque. He got seven bottles. That left the rest to be lugged around to sell. The next stop was a soft-drink shop with one lone man inside. He was approached and went to a backroom, returning to tell the two to speak to the boss, a woman. She tried to chisel the price but the two would not deal with her. They left for the pool-parlour across the street.

The boss came out, a friendly man, asking the name of each of the two men and the town from which they came. After receiving the required information he announced that he was playing pool with a namesake of one man and would introduce him. After a few minutes they (with the same name) came to the front and told the two to wait until he brought his car to take what they had. While they were waiting a friend of the man in the soft-drink shop beckoned them to follow him to his room in a hotel and he bought the remainder. They left the hotel to wait for the man with the car. When he was told that they had no more on them but could get some from the ship, he drove them down to the dock.

The night was dark. A fine rain was falling, as the two went to get the two bottles requested. As it was in the month of November, the river was low. One man went to the lower landing while the other went through the warehouse at street-level. The goods were handed to the one on the quay who went right away to consummate the deal. His accomplice went the longer route by going the way he had come. When he was approaching the car he saw two figures grab his partner, then he was caught, also.

They were Revenue Officers who ordered all three to accompany them to the ship then they were taken to the First Mate's cabin to be interrogated. The first question asked of the one man was, calling his name, "Where did you get this whiskey?"

The surprise answer came, "Sir, this is my cousin and I was asked to pay him a visit if I ever got out this way."

Without hesitation, the Mate then asked of the supposed cousin his name. It was the same, producing a calling card to substantiate it. The missing whiskey from the cargo had not been discovered at this stage. During these short proceedings one Revenue Officer left to search the crew's quarters. All he did was to turn over the pillows in the bunks of the two, then telling the men in the forecastle that two of their men had been caught bootlegging and would be taken for a hearing ashore.

The Mate was informed with the promise that they would be back in time to sail in the morning. All five left the ship by way of the gangway leading to the warehouse that was dimly lighted. Then they were herded into a dark corner where one of the bottles was opened and passed among the three of them, as the two seamen were total abstainers. After a couple of rounds, one Revenue Officer spoke up, stating that he had to make the pinch because the woman who owned the soft-drink shop made the charge that they had ten bottles in their pockets yet they were clean when caught. He was not interested as to their disappearance and had no intention of further apprehension. So he went to the telephone to tell the woman that he had the two-lawbreakers and allowed one of them to say something as proof of their being detained. As for the buyer of the two bottles that were now being disintegrated, he had lost out and was offered his money back but he refused. Talking, drinking and time went on until both bottles were emptied. Then a question was asked of the bootleggers,

"This stuff is good. Is there more on your ship? I want to bring a bottle home with me."

The two bootleggers went into a huddle, one went to the lower landing the other went aboard and passed three bottles ashore, one for each of the two Revenue Officers and the customer, thus ending the trial.

When the two got in the forecastle they received some well-earned cussing because at the beginning of the trip the hat was passed around to buy some booze to celebrate the holidays; Christmas and New Year, with the boatswain taking charge of it. It resulted in the first holiday taking all there was of it; even though the teetotalers paid their share, that was not sufficient to excuse them from not producing some of what they had for the New Year's anticipated celebration.

In order not to delay the sailing the Old Man paid a fine of sixty-five dollars. Each night that we were in that port he entertained a woman who, when leaving, required assistance to enter the cab that was ordered for her to return home in an intoxicated condition. Perhaps she did not like his booze or its after-effects to cause her to turn him in. Probably her husband did; he would not enjoy her company in that state. In either event the next morning before sailing, the Old Man was arrested when he went ashore carrying one bottle of wine.

For the rest of the fourth trip in this large "Rum-Runner," nothing of consequence happened but I was fortunate in being at the wheel near the end, as we were steaming through the Straits of Dover on a clear sunny morning, with the coasts of France and England in clear view. On Cape Griz Nez, a monument had been erected looking to the white-cliffs of Dover, where bluebirds do not fly. It is doubtful if ever they did, but a facsimile of a bluebird was there now with the words "Lest We Forget." Just inside the Dover Harbour entrance that grim reminder of numerous, needless deaths, was still there, six years later; the H.M.S. Gorgan. Her bilges were sometimes referred to as blisters because of the wide-beam of Monitors still visible for miles. As it was the forenoon, the Third Mate's watch, I asked him to put the glasses on it to get a good view. He asked if I knew what it was. I told him the gruesome story; the reason in all probability for her still lying there may have been for the danger that still existed. At the time of her demise she was loaded with sixteen-inch shells. Maybe the bluebirds came to nest there.

The loss of three cases of whiskey was discovered in Vancouver. For that reason when we reached home shores, none of us were permitted to ship out again because some unknown person or persons knew how to fool the Customs in America, as the builders and owners had done. It meant that I would have to pack up my worldly possessions and go vessel searching once again. No sooner had I went ashore in Dover than all the old feelings in me surfaced. Will I ever find my own anchor?

The next tub I went to sea in was a trunk-ship-collier, owned as usual by a member of Parliament to support the Seamen's Union members from getting too much out of life and it could hardly be classified as a ship. No coal was being mined in England at this time due to the miners' strike. Therefore, this tub must have been taken out of mothballs to act as a "strike-breaker;" first going to St. Johns, Cape Breton Islands for bunkers, then proceeding to Baltimore to load coal for Dublin, Ireland.

Although no one in charge actually called the men aboard "dogs," the treatment for them was comparable to the same. Each man was getting his daily ration of one pail of water for drinking, if need be; for shaving, brushing teeth, washing his body, work clothes, underwear and eating utensils; then letting it stand in the forecastle for twenty-four hours where ten crew members ate and slept. That was standard operational procedure. But when the sailors and firemen are put on an isolated rock containing the ruins of a fort in the Baltimore Harbour, staying for hours on a hot July day with absolutely no protection from the sun while the ship was being fumigated, this is enough inconvenience. The walls did not provide any shade because one could not go near them. There were no sanitary facilities and there was much evidence that this was not the first crew to be subjected to this kind of treatment.

There was one of two choices available; either getting sunburned or soaking in the surrounding water that was stinking and dirty. Most of us chose the latter for the greater part of the time, even by those who could not swim. One could not swim in this water without getting its taste and for days following when we bent to do something, that water would drip from our noses.

As the result of the men being placed in these conditions, the agent for the company and the Old Man would have to share the amount of money that was billed to the owner for an extra sixteen meals from a hotel.

It is doubtful that the American Authorities knew of these conditions. Their war on rats was being waged with success. It would be logical to also assume that war would be fought against diseases that unsanitary conditions breed.

10

I Give Up the Sea

The more I saw of England's worsening conditions the more discontent I became in this land of "opportunity for all." America had also lost many men during that war to end all wars. That new land also had a very high death toll due to the pandemic Influenza disease that traveled across the ocean to its shores. Yet those on the casualty list in England who had survived with the loss of a limb or limbs, already had their pensions reduced by half to help pay the war debt. At no time did I nurture any anarchistic thoughts because I have the highest admiration and respect for the Royal Family-knowing full well that my condition was not due to them. When this trip ended, I was determined not to go to sea again. Again, the question arose, what to do?

Having finished with the sea due to frustration and disgust, there arose now the problem of fitting in somewhere that required unskilled labour, outside of working in a rigging loft where an opening could never be found. The trips made to the West Coast of America had benefited me in the best way imaginable-mentally and physically. At this time on one run to that part of the country, it was quite noticeable to the foreigner that physical culture played a great part in the lifestyle of the people. It was puzzling to me as to what gave these people their erect bearing, squared shoulders, thick necks and developed biceps, while at this time I was plagued with stomach trouble brought on by the monotonous diet of the Union and the Grand Hotel, followed by the years at sea where diets were not taken into consideration.

Without seeking medical advice I took it upon myself to find a cure. Each morning I took one-half teaspoon of Epsom Salts before each morning meal, with a quarter teaspoon of table salt; then once each week five teaspoons of the former into a half glass of water. This required my going amidst-ship for this special order. It was handed to me in a way not done for others, as drinking water was not included in the water ration. It is doubtful that the ship's complement who inhabited this exclusive part of the ship would see a seaman die of thirst. They would first close their eyes.

This condition existed until the day a visitor from the "Mission to Seamen" brought a large number of Physical Culture magazines. Upon opening the first one there was a one-page article with the caption, "How I Cured My Indigestion In Three Days." That one little article was so convincing to make me try the cure, requiring about ten minutes each day, with absolutely no cost whatsoever. During the third day the discomfort was the worst it had ever been but the next day it left me and did not return, so I stuck to the culture; improving each day in the development of the little there was of me.

As my physical condition improved it was noticed by several acquaintances when I returned to England. I was aided in my quest to end my sea-faring days by a group of young men of the Sunday School, across the street from where I lived. They asked me to be their physical health instructor. When it became known to them that the sea was my livelihood, one among them told me that his father could get me a job in the town. This man, it so turned out, was on the Council, so I was to get a job through political pull.

The next morning I reported to the contractor's foreman who is building houses of concrete blocks that are being made on an all sand site. A shovel is handed to me to dig a trench for the footings of not more than six inches deep where the stakes are put and gradually lessening the depth to four inches between them. Having done that for one hour, I am then put to mixing the concrete for the foundation: with a mix of nine wheelbarrows of aggregate to one bag of cement, but when the inspector is not around, make it thirteen to one; also, instead of turning the dry mix over three times to make do with two times.

There are two of us to do this work but at the end of the first half-day I am without a partner, who, although much huskier than I, could not take it. For two weeks following, not one man does more than one day on this job. So there are days that I have this job alone, acquired with political pull and being turned down by those who do not have such benefits. It requires that one mixer has to fill the barrow, then wheel the stuff to the shallow trenches. Having been through the mill it did not bother me as much as it does the one who is assisting me, when the masons call for mud. A fair day's work is being done for the money.

One day when I am working alone, cement is needed, so the two masons have to go for it. Taking advantage of the situation I keep wheeling aggregate to the mixing-board until there are eighteen barrows full for the last bag of cement. In this way I am able to get a little breather and at the same time not pay any particular attention as to who is watching-providing it is not the inspector.

In the local paper of that week there appeared a column of criticism regarding the construction on work being done for this borough, to the effect that the writer, a retired doctor, would on no account accept these houses even with a cash payment to do so.

There was no sense in continuing this work when one night of the week was devoted to instruct and demonstrate physical culture; doing exercises that were tiring, with aching limbs, to the point where the rings felt more like bar-bells. Then the thought entered my mind that somewhere in this world there was a country where an outcast could get more than what had been put in my path in appreciation of service. It meant going back to sea for transportation, retracting my vow never to go again. At least it would be for only a one-way trip, to a place unknown to me as yet.

The next morning I boarded the first train to Manchester. Upon arriving there I made a beeline to the shipping-office where, by a stroke of luck, I met a former resident of Fleetwood. After his enquiring as to the nature of my business, he took me to meet the Shipping-Master, who telephoned the Locks in the Manchester Ship Canal and inquired as to what ship was coming through and the time it would reach the dock and where it would berth. He then wrote a note for me to give to the First Mate, to ensure my getting a job. As the Shipping Master would not know until the time of signing on the crew, where the ship was going, my destination was also unknown. I thought it would be fair to tell him what my intentions were.

After I had related briefly the reason, he put the reply in two beautiful words, "Good-Luck."

Everything went according to schedule. I was signed on two days later then sailed on the following day. The reading of the articles contained the words I most wanted to hear, when it was announced that the first port of call was Antwerp, Belgium. That was of no interest to me but then Boston, Brooklyn, New Zealand and Australia were. Here were a number of choices yet only one was needed. It was either Brooklyn or a port in Australia. If Australia where by the remotest chance, would I get to meet another Commander who wanted me to make a home with him?

The time came to sail. I was determined that it would be the last trip. In looking back without regret as to the way that time was spent yet at the same time reflecting upon with whom it was spent; I reached some realizations. I had known men of all statures with different philosophies but the ones that intrigued me the most among all my shipmates were those unkempt characters who frequented the waterfront.

This area of my world produced some of that kind as part of the crew of a tanker. In one Dogwatch two crewmembers were relating their experiences while sitting on a locker in the forecastle, in not much above a whisper. Both were experienced windjammer sailors, judging by their naming the rigging of the vessels. One was telling the other where he had seen some of the ships mentioned, with my being the sole listener as I lay in my bunk above them.

One told of his experiences in the Spanish Navy as coxswain of the Admiral launch, even though he was from Liverpool but with his being a crewmember with other nationals, he had a knowledge of the languages. The other man told of his being in the Italian Navy, then in the Argentine Navy. He claimed to be a Canadian but he had been a drifter in so many countries that he was a citizen of none.

The Englishman told of his joining a Windjammer in San Francisco that needed an entire crew. It turned out to be quite a motley throng of many tongues, including Scandinavians and Chileans. One of the former came aboard well dressed with a gold watch and chain across his vest. This brought a covetous look from the eyes of those around, especially from the last mentioned. After a few days at sea the owner of the wealth fell from a yardarm. According to the narrator, as soon as he hit the deck a Chilean went to that man's locker emptying it of all its possessions. This was not unusual behaviour for him (the Chilean) nor was his fetish of superstition.

The Englishman, knowing this, would constantly remind the thief that the dead man would haunt him all the time he had this loot; that he should do the right thing and give back those things. Day after day he would work on this man's conscience and each time that he was on the verge of conceding he would then back out.

One night when the ship was in the doldrums, the thief was on the lookout pacing the catwalk across the forecastle head. The night was very dark. The storyteller was the helmsman and as there was not a breath of air, no steering could be done. He crept forward to watch the lookout space from port to starboard and back again with an occasional pause to look straight ahead. Taking advantage of the darkness he could get within arm's length without being noticed so he waited until the opportunity came for him to get fore-side of the catwalk. Once there he waited in a crouch for when the lookout would stop in the middle to look ahead. To him in the crouch it seemed that he was in for a disappointment but at long last that moment came. As soon as it did he jumped up in front of him, scaring him to the point that without hesitation, he took a leap overboard. The chap had been told so often that the man who fell from the yardarm would haunt him for the rest of his life or until he surrendered that man's belongings and he didn't take it with a pinch of salt but rather with an ocean of salt-water.

At the end of that watch there was a new owner of the expensive suit and watch. He also could not account for the lookout being missing when it came to relieve, as the night was so dark it proved to be a perfect alibi. The riches that were purloined would be exchanged either directly or indirectly for drink; the mainstay of life for this human derelict. His sole possessions were one pair of dungarees, two pairs of "T" shirts and shorts, with one pair being carried in the pockets of an American Navy pea-jacket and one pair of sandals.

My observations were that those two story-swapping men were the best of friends and good shipmates.

11

My Last Shipmate

Every seaport has an element of mankind near its waterfront walking around unkempt, filthy-looking, and most of the time, soused. They do not hesitate to ask you for money to buy a cup of coffee. Show them the money then ask them for the coffee and you will without a doubt, get a flow of the best nautical profanity as smooth as, "Afton Waters," or by way of being different ask them to change five dollars then check your identification card to see if the names correspond with those you have been called. To judge these characters as being "no good" is a stupid mistake.

First of all, they are not in the rat race; that is, the self-imposed pressure those labour under in order to strive for more than what they have. More likely these characters of doubtful worth can be counted on not to do anything unfair to you thereby making for good company once at sea. These men are drinkers but not alcoholics because they go to sea once the source of supply runs out and once there, they dry out and become quiet, inoffensive and clean within the limits afforded. Some of the unusual happenings that these men have experienced make for some very interesting reading of comedy or tragedy. As a result they do not take living as a serious matter. This type of man was the last shipmate of mine. I talked him into jumping ship in these United States, and joining him a week later with the intention of trying to get him to go my way.

We were entirely opposites, with his being a bum who lived to drink, while I was a bum who did not drink but just tried to live.. Instead, I was a physical culturist.

The trip began at Salford on the Manchester Ship Canal. The ship was a nine thousand ton freighter. Her name will not be mentioned in the hope of forgetting all the sooner. She was one vessel that had no regular route and was chartered by other companies, therefore she was void of comforts in all respects; even to heat in the forecastle, with little water as usual and a minimum of food, all of poor quality.

These conditions existed less than ten years after the war to end all wars yet in such circumstances it was a damn good reason to start another war but there was a problem with whom to fight. However, we kept the peace and continued our cleaning habits in a filthy fashion because there was a lack of choice. Alas, we could still be classified as stinkers.

Late in November in the year 1926 we sailed, bound for the ports that were read to us in the Articles. Slowly we went to the first port of call, with a record-dash without splash, at less than five knots an hour. It became apparent that this ship was not going to increase its speed, for one reason only. She was a coal-burner with Arab firemen. These men knew that they could not get their jobs without having two pound notes in their hands, leaving same on board after applying. Based on the fact the ownership gets transferred to them once at sea, their philosophy was, "More days, more dollars." So be advised, should one be looking for a slow boat to China, to look for these two qualities.

These men shared the forecastle with the deckhands, separated only by a tongue and groove partition. That made it possible to hear noises from each side. Such was the case after being at sea a few days, when one of the firemen was caught cheating at cards during the first dogwatch. Then all Hell let loose, so it seemed, because they threw the small coal stove at one another and everything else that could be loosened. We waited in expectation of seeing something or somebody come through the partition uninvited.

Now that bum friend of mine by name of Jock McCrossin, had sailed many times with these nationals who were causing this upheaval. He knew how to cope with the problem if one did come through, in this way. He advised us to follow him and to pick up a hatch batten, then sit and wait for the first one to enter.

Shortly afterwards, quiet was restored without intrusion. Then it dawned on me that we had obeyed the orders of this man who but a few days before had come aboard drunk and dirty, with nothing resembling a sea-kit, like a typical bum. Yet his concern was for our safety because he knew that the quarrelers would have no consideration for anyone who happened to be in their path. Also at his suggestion, we were to go on deck at eight bells to look at the casualties. When lo and behold, the four men who were to relieve the watch in the stoke-hold were literally a bloody mess.

At Antwerp we took on five thousand tons of cement that would make us nicely ballasted to cross the Atlantic during the month of December. Having left on the December 4, 1926, bound for Boston; arriving there January 8, 1927, was a mere thirty-five days later. No bad weather had delayed us, which is most unusual for that time of the year. It was due entirely to the firemen counting the money that they were going to make and who probably needed plenty of time to do just that.

Three weeks after leaving Antwerp, no one up to this time, had been detailed to clean the forecastle; the compartment where ten men ate, smoked, bathed, slept and spent time during dogwatches to bat the breeze.

After hearing so much about this self-nominated "Devil" who boasted of his coming from a place in a remote part of Scotland, that none of us had heard of or would ever see. I told Jock when we were alone that I had been there on more than one occasion. It was agreed that I should call this guy's bluff and also to take it upon ourselves to clean the quarters for the first time in a month.

That evening as soon as the "blowhard" went into his bragging session, I interrupted, to inform him of my having been in his hometown but he expressed his doubts in a vulgar manner. I had been there in a steam trawler where we would go when being chased by the fisheries' gunboat for poaching. This place was land-locked and afforded good shelter in bad weather. It had a quay with a hotel built of solid granite, close by. Within a short distance was the village. In the middle of it was a small bridge that divided Inver from Loch Inver. To convince him of the truth in what was said, the name of the hotel manager was mentioned, the widowed mother of the only two teachers in the local school. To convince him further there was a picture of myself with a shipmate on the widow's mantelpiece, given to her when we brought her fish that all five of us would eat for supper.

Her husband was a casualty of the war. He was decorated for bravery while serving with a famous Scottish regiment. On the quay was a stone that no one passed without sitting on it because it was on this stone that Sir Walter Scott sat to write his well known poem, "Lochinvar."

After the boatswain heard this he went to his cabin without a word. That left us with the pleasant knowledge that he would not tell us of the last ninety years of his youthful escapades in a place that did not have one store. All supplies were brought in by mail-boat.

The next morning instead of turning to on deck at his command, Jock and I cleaned the forecastle. Here then was another instance where a bum stood by; in him I had a shipmate and a much valued friend.

The reason for not putting men to clean the quarters was to conserve water. The amount allotted for this chore is two pails of it each Wednesday and Saturday; generally this was the rule on all freighters. But this one was going so damn slow that she could have been mistaken for a landmark or suspected of being boarded as a derelict. This problem of loitering on the Atlantic was at last getting the Old Man to worry, so he ordered the First Mate to tell all the experienced firemen who were among the deck-hands, to go below to do the firing of the boilers. He was reluctant to do this because that would leave him short-handed to get the paint chipped, scraped and painted again.

All the men in the forecastle had seen active service with the exception of Jock and an asthmatic foreigner. They did not expect their country to do anything for them but they did not bargain for conditions such as these.

Actually then, we served the country for what? To be subjected to conditions such as those experienced in war; to be exploited by the government. When one gets the opportunity to spend a vacation during the bleak month of December on the Atlantic Ocean, there is ample time to sit and think of what the future has in store. Should one follow such an un-diversified career as this?

In our motley crew there were two more Scots besides the boatswain but they isolated themselves. So Jock and I got better acquainted as the trip wore on. We had been to sea long enough to be fed up with looking at the same faces each day. Since the evening of the disturbance over the card-game there had been calm because the stove was smashed. Since there was no heat, there was no alternative but to turn in. These men now became a problem for the Skipper to solve. Once again he put the squeeze on the First Mate to weed out the experienced firemen from the seamen's forecastle because the speed as yet had not reached five knots an hour.

From the discharge books in his possession while at sea he had access to the information he needed to find out who had done firing. From that data he discovered two, who incidentally, were none other than Jock and me.

Knowing what was coming our way, Jock tipped me off to refuse for two reasons; one was that it was not an emergency and the other for personal safety. He then went on to relate an experience in one ship in similar circumstances. The Mate's idea was to put only one of us in a firing watch in order to push things along. A good thought if it could be put into practice, which was most unlikely. Jock told of a man who had done this and all seemed to go well during the first watch until it was time to go off and just as he showed his head above the top landing he was dealt a heavy blow, causing him to fall from the ladder, unconscious.

Sailors were assigned to get the man up and put him in his bunk until he came around. That was enough of a determent to stop others from doing the same and for the next few days nothing was done in retaliation just to lull the Arabs into a false sense of pride and security. Then one dark night a planned campaign was put into operation. It called for the last man entering the stokehold from each side of the ship to be grabbed, their hands placed on a hatch and to be beaten to a pulp with steel bars.

I did not relish the idea of being treated roughly. When I was ordered to go below to fire, I gave a flat refusal for the reason Jock had provided. I was smaller than Jock in stature, so it was logical to assume that he would not be told to go because he would not hesitate to tell the Mate to oscillate that part of his anatomy that was better hidden, even if "please" was the last word of the request.

Jock, although a bum, respected authority and obeyed orders within reason. He took his good old time in doing so. For instance, the mate wanted a reading from the log. Jock was on standby when the mate blew his whistle, first once, then twice, then a third time before Jock showed up. When he did, the mate told him he had blown the whistle three times.

The reply he got was, "Jesus Christ, you can count that much and do you know that once more will make four?"

The mate let him know that he wanted a reading on time each hour, to record the speed. Jock once reminded him that he should not worry because he said, "This son of a bitch ain't going no place." That was true as the recorded speed still showed less than five knots.

Day after day, the sea and the sky were the same colour; grey, so if land was near it would be difficult to see but I never gave up looking for it while on the lookout. I was passing the time by singing and talking to the porpoises, even to calling them by name, which seemed to give me the impression that they responded. Ofttimes I had seen them at a distance but when a musical instrument was played they would gather around the bow, weaving and leaping, exhaling a small spray from their heads.

At least I had the satisfaction of knowing that there was an America because I had been there. I was returning to it very slowly, as it so happened was an advantage. More days meant more dollars and would enable me to make a larger draw against my pay, when the time for leaving came. Also, there was Jock to sustain. He had drawn to the limit in Antwerp to enable him to begin the second part of the trip, drunk.

The dogwatches were spent each day in one fashion; with all of us huddled around the small stove, listening attentively to an episode that was of interest in the lives of each one. One man was at Hill 60 in France, when the Prime Minister stood on a bridge in London to hear of its being leveled with explosives, to stop its use as an observation post by the enemy. When my turn came, the action on the Dover Patrol was revived. Jock had not done active service because of failing sight but he had served in the Merchant Marine.

Jock was not talkative but on this particular evening when he decided to talk we were all ears. He went on to say that he was on the ship that was the nearest to the collision that caused the Halifax explosion. Up to that time it was one of the biggest on record. For one to be that close is nothing short of a miracle to live to tell it.

He started by saying, "My ship is at anchor in this harbour. We're all there working on deck. The chap standing next to me gives a quick call for us to pay attention. We look up an' I bloody well do not want to believe what my poor eyes see," Jock pauses to force down the rising tone of his emotion, "this ship is only a few hops-and-jumps away from us but we can see it's damned sure set on a collision course with another in the harbour. That whole ship's company grabs for life-boats and they're pulling like hell for the shore. My crewmates start lining the port-rail to wait for the crash that's impossible to avoid. I'm not really in the mood for this coming gore so I tell the one next to me that I'm going below to roll a cigarette and to call me when it's over. My mate says he will and asks me to roll one for him.

"At this time there is only one man in the forecastle. He is sleeping because he took the anchor watch all night. Just as I finish rolling the second cigarette and about to go back on deck with it, the crash comes.

"This whole event makes headline-news, I know because I read it but the details I just told you men weren't included in print. For instance, where my crewmates were lining the portside of our ship just a few minutes before, alive and well, they're now lined the starboard handrails in bits. The force of the explosion blew them straight across the deck and through the railing, leaving parts of their humanity sticking on the railings. Like minnow slipping through a trawl-line".

One of us now asks Jock his reason for not taking advantage of the opportunity to claim something for himself He responds, "I am very lucky to survive." Furthermore, he admits, "I would be spending that money for drink and when it's all gone I would be back here just the same." As a result of his way of thinking, he would be classified as being a bloody fool. He then was not a bum of a man but more likely a man of a bum.

After hearing his story, I vowed that if at all possible, I would do all in my power to help him, should he be in need. He was never asked if this in any way had changed him from what society would call the average human being into his present being and way of life. At no time did he ask for anything personal of us, so why should we of him? As he told his story, not a sound came from the fire-men's side; not that they could not have heard enough to become interested, but because it must have been too cold for them to do anything but turn in. As it was, our condensed breaths were freezing inside the forecastle and hereafter a fire was kept in the whole time.

The days following were plain routine that warranted our remembering nothing until the thirty-fifth day after leaving Antwerp. At long last an Atlantic crossing had been made by what was classed as a modern steam-vessel in record time, not with any reference to high-speed but on the contrary.

Boston proved to be a haven for us, although the temperature was hovering around zero with rather thick fog on the ground. We moored at the Army Base. Shortly afterward an elderly Scotsman from the Mission for Seamen came to us to extend an invitation to visit it. Glad for the change and the break in monotony, at least I was expecting to spend an evening of hymn singing with a group and to be in a place that would be warm.

To my surprise the first three items on that evening's programme were: The National Anthem, the same tune for both the countries at the time, the Invocation followed with a recitation by this aforementioned Scotsman, who had spent his younger years in British ships. It was a long poem of the sea and a windjammer, slightly exaggerated with sound effects produced by the audience. One would never tire of hearing it no matter how often it was told in that way. It served as the opener for the entertainment provided by people of the theatre; followed by dancing, with teachers for the awkward squad and refreshments. This was fifty years ago, so somewhat late, still I wish to thank the people of Boston who gave so much of themselves to help us outsiders and with a look skyward I say, "Thanks to a Grand Old Scot."

For nine consecutive evenings I boarded the streetcar bound for the best Mission I had ever visited. I dressed in a light grey suit with no topcoat, in bitter cold weather. Although I was stared at by many and was probably looked upon as a nut, there was a reason for this scant attire. At the time of signing on in Salford, the Articles were read aloud by the Shipping Master without his seeming to mention that this ship would call at American ports on its voyage from Europe to Australasia. Therefore the crew was of the opinion that we would make this trip in Summer-like climate, so we did not prepare for cold weather. Seamen like to pick ships that dodge the Winter-more so, if one had not seen that kind of weather in five years, as in my case. The American winters that I had experienced on the West Coast were much milder than this one. Add to that the two winters I spent going to the Near East. Temperatures there could reach sky-high proportions. It was very hot in Persia to the extent that when I returned to England I was forced to wear an overcoat in July, as my teeth kept making castanet noises. I was told it was because my blood system had not been re-acclimated. Coincidentally, Persia had not changed its name to Iran as yet. She would wait another handful of years to make it official.

Now I was feeling the cold but my regular exercises were standing me in good stead. For this I give thanks to the "Mission to Seamen in San Francisco" for its Physical Culture Magazines. If one can become accustomed to living in the cold like those eleven years I had spent at Paupers' Mansion, perhaps it was why I did not become ill with lung fluids as had some crewmembers. During a very heavy snowstorm, accompanied with high velocity winds, we left Boston headed for Brooklyn. Upon arriving, the forecastle was unloaded of six men who were put into ambulances. Jock went along on the pretense of also being sick with pneumonia. It had been arranged between us to provide him with the opportunity to find a room for the both of us, with money supplied by me. He had no money coming to him because he had made advances against his pay to the limit in each of the ports we stayed.

I trusted him and he did the right thing. He came down to dockside to tell me that he had found quarters and also a job. It was agreed that I would stay aboard another week, make another advance then join him.

New York in the winter was considered to be a tough place to find a job but we each found one the day following, after jumping ship. For a few weeks ashore Jock behaved then he got the urge to go to sea again. He shipped out in an American ship on a trip that lasted only six weeks. He was paid off and got drunk. That was during prohibition and then he was rolled. Late on a Saturday afternoon he came to where I was working and confessed to me what he had done. He then ended by saying that he was sailing at midnight on a British freighter bound for China.

We spent the remaining time together, with my begging him to change his mind by promising that I would stand by him, regardless, but without success. I had trusted him and he had done the right thing by me but not for himself. He was adamant and refused the offer. He said that I had already done enough for him and that he knew he did not have the capability to repay and that I should forget him. Close to midnight we walked the streets together, leading to the Brooklyn waterfront. The only sounds were our footsteps on the pavements of this deserted section.

When getting to where the ship was moored, our companionship ended with a handshake and a final plea for him to change his mind. With an expression of thanks for all that I had done for him, including the kit-bag with its contents that was slung over his shoulder, his last words, with the Scottish burr, "Good-bye,

Shorty, stay in America, it is much better." This was the parting of the last ship-mate of mine.

The sea had no further attraction for me, as I had found a job in this country. Although it was considered menial it was the highest paid one that I had ever had and being eighty dollars a month. For even this, God Bless America. A feeling of loneliness came over me when Jock had left but had he accepted my offer, I knew as we sat eating our last meal together, watching him closely, that before long he would prove to be a burden. He must have also known it and that probably was his main reason for leaving. He was losing his sight rapidly and before long he would not see me again, had he stayed.

Jock, if ever you learn to read Braille, God willing, you read this.

12

Lost Waif Is No More

After all the years of being alone, the aloneness was always in my mind, thinking it had to be this way for two reasons. One was that I was assumed to be an illegal alien; the other was caused by the lack of information regarding myself, if in the event that I ever should take an oath to love, honour and obey. What could I tell any woman of my background? Why would she want to believe me when by jumping ship and settling here in the customary manner might be the source of my capture? I had no skills aside from fishing and fighting. I had nothing to offer. The opportunity to remain in this country meant a great deal to me. At this time I thought that being so far from where I was brought up, I could see no possibility of my ever finding the clues that would lead to my identity. Although I desired to know who I am; from whence I was born and if I had any known living relatives, I also needed to make a way for myself in this most alluring country. But amongst all these questions, at the top of my mental list was what name I should use? In the event of being questioned by bobbies for infractions of any American rules and not know what name to give, left me in a precarious juxtaposition.

Affixed to my identification card was the name, Herrington Heard. Although it was a typical British name, I did not look it, but my dialect would give me away. Years at sea had confirmed me to a swarthy colour, yet as a kid in Paupers' Mansion there was rare times for absorbing sunshine, I still had a slighter tan covering. Fortunately, I never developed sea-boils, instead, mal-de-mer stayed with me for most of my years at watery employ.

Another trivial matter was that after spending all those years in Dover, my naval discharge papers lists me as living in Fleetwood, thanks to the loan of my superior's address given to the Wren.

The idea of working in a restaurant kitchen as a dishwasher may not have impressed anyone, yet I was impressed. I earned more money each month than I ever had in England, and the meals were to my liking. In brief time I was able to expand my career opportunities to include door-to-door sales, waitering in the Catskills and operating a strictly coffee business in Manhattan.

By now I was known as Harry Heard because Mornington seemed not to suit my Yankee customers or me. The business consisted of brewing fresh pots of coffee, Mondays through Fridays; to be hand delivered to the construction workmen assembling the city's skyscrapers. I teamed up with an Irishman about my age. Together we took turns in brewing our gold then walking the steel girders to deliver the blue enamel pots and collect the profits. I was able to carry six pots of the steaming stuff on each run.

"Oh, get off it Harry, do I have to kick your arse to get you going?"

"Thank you, no. Go enjoy your New Year's party."

"I promised Jeannie and Andy and you're not going to make me break my promise."

This conversation took place with my coffee partner, Mike. Threatening to throw me over his shoulder convinced me to don the new grey suit I had bought that previous autumn and do as I was told. I refrained from admitting to him, my inexperience in "party going" but then listening to a radio on this holiday eve lost its luster. And so I went with Mike and have never regretted it since.

The quiet young woman with hazel eyes and shining brown hair welcomed me by extending her small hand while wishing me holiday greetings. I repeated her name, "Josephine Conroy," took her hand, and never let go.

I did take that oath and married one whom there was understanding and compassion. That was forty-eight years ago. God has blessed us with three children, twelve grandchildren and two great-grandchildren. For this we thank Thee, O Lord.

At the time those many years ago, sadness was my number one monster to combat. Regardless of all those past existing unpleasant conditions, there was always another topic of discussion; me and from where did I come? The only information I could give my wife were the contents of two statements, both conflicting. One came from the Dover Union, Paupers' Mansion; the other from the Constables in that town of Dover. These were obtained following my ordered expulsion from the Naval Office and at the time of filing those discharge papers.

The contents of these statements I gave to my wife verbally, who had faith in me to decide to follow these leads once after obtaining copies to these effects, if that was possible after so many years. At her suggestion, my wife and I decided to take the matter to an attorney whom we thought would have the capability of obtaining affidavits. He then advised us as to what steps to take toward my becoming an American citizen. It turned out that this step was futile, as he was advised by the Constables (Dover Police in England) to seek the services of a private detective from their area. The name of one detective was conveniently suggested in the letter.

That response so angered my gentle Josie that she decided to write that department with the threat to sue in the event it did not supply the information requested. Some days later she received a prompt reply that corresponded with one of the two statements I had provided. She then took this to the attorney who was curious as to its contents and he requested the opportunity to pursue this matter further.

When I told him what the Constables' record was on me, he said, "If I had not known your wife I would think you are crazy."

He was going to direct inquiries back to the Dover Police in reference to the letter from them to the effect that I was brought to them from Berne, Switzerland. That I was the waif found on the high seas seemed quite dubious. When Josie researched all of the Spanish speaking countries, she found one in Middle America known as the Switzerland of the Western Hemisphere; land of the Quetzal where it provides pleasure for the rich.

Guatemala, Central America, was where England's source of quinine derived from the bark of the cinchona tree plantations was, she had many holdings and even took a chunk of the country that they re-named, British Honduras;. Nothing made sense! Was this a very sick joke played on my parents and me?

While this correspondence was being carried on, Josie frequently rode the subway from Brooklyn to the New York City Public Library, looking for clues in old newspapers around the turn of the century, pertaining to births and deaths of persons with either of the names produced by the two institutions. She had persevered in her quest to the point that the librarian would expect her and have ready whatever was available for that period.

However, rather than disappoint her entirely, he (the librarian) had waiting for her on one particular day, a copy of the Paris edition of the London Daily Graphic. In it was the clue we sought.

The caption in the paper read: "Lost Waif," April of 1904, with a picture of the boy found on the steps of the Madelaine Church in Paris, France. It was me in my specially made sailor outfit and overcoat, with the same hat I had worn on Sundays at Paupers' Mansion. The moment of truth was upon me and I was too numbed with these findings.

The significance in that name, Madelaine Church, is that later in her research, my wife discovered there was an exact replica of that building in Guatemala City. The newspaper reported that this boy was not able to speak English or French; he was questioned in many languages but never in Spanish, hence they nicknamed him Frenchy. The description of the clothes he was wearing tallied to a "T" with what an elderly inmate had also told me at the Dover Union that I wore when admitted. It was thought that my mother might have been an actress, the French newspaper reported. That was in April of 1904.

Is it not a coincidence and questionable when at the same time a little boy answering the same description and in similar circumstances is reported by the Dover Police to have been abandoned in Berne, Switzerland at the same time as the boy in Paris? Also, according to the Times Picayune of New Orleans, Louisiana, a girl was said to be the daughter of the President General José Maria Reyna Barrios and his wife, Algeria of New Orleans. She was the same age as Lost Waif and said to be abandoned in Paris and placed in an English convent.

If the latter was true, can it be substantiated? As that girl was not publicized nor could her mother have abandoned her because she was being incarcerated in England and could not defend herself. Further details shall follow but I must first begin with myself.

The day following the upheaval I innocently caused by my telling the truth in that naval war of words at the discharge office caused me to look for answers. I went back to the Union that day to make inquiries about myself; to that squat person who had wanted me to complete the probation sentence. She came to greet me, asking the nature of my business. Without standing on ceremony I demanded a statement in writing as to the reason for my being committed and the whereabouts of my parents. She took me into another room and, opened a large book of records. In it, concerning me, was one simple entry:

Errington Herd. Born on the High Sea.

At the time that specific day so long ago, it was not visiting hours, regardless, I went to the Infirmary to question some of the male patients who were there when I was admitted. They remembered the incident well but could not give any further information beyond my being dressed in a sailor suit and speaking Spanish and being isolated in the Infirmary without being ill. I then went to the Doctor who gave me the same answers but did admit to naming me Frenchy.

From there I went to the police, stating to the one on duty, "I am Errington Herd. I was committed to the Dover Union in April of 1904 and would like information concerning myself and parents whom I have not seen since."

Without lifting his eyes from what he was perusing, he simply said, "Come back in three days."

At the appointed time I returned for information requested and was handed a statement enclosed in a plain envelope that read:

"On April 21st of 1904, a boy named Mornington Heard was brought from Berne, Switzerland to Dover by Sgt. Detective Michel of the Swiss Police Department. He was abandoned, presumably of English parents. He was taken to the Dover Union."

Upon receiving this statement I asked advice of the man at the desk as to what I should do next. He suggested my writing to the British Consul in Berne.

The reply from him (the British Consul in Berne) came to the effect that he regretted being unable to supply the desired information but he had no record of it.

"My Gawd, Harry, who's the biggest liar?" The newspapers give you no name, the Dover Police say you're Mornington Heard and that Orphanage says you're Errington Herd, but for the eleven years there no one says this name and you're called Froggie at school!"

"I do not know what to think. It's been so long ago." I grinned but felt depressed, "but thanks to you dear, we have eliminated the Swiss from the equation."

"Wait, just a minute. Don't you dare say you're giving up?"

"I feel it is useless to continue searching after receiving such conflicting affidavits," tearing them up before submitting the pieces to the trash.

"Well, I'm not!"

"Please Josie, it is too much to handle. Let us just drop it. We have our lives to get on with."

"Darned right we do and that's why I'm going to keep researching for the answers. You bet I'm curious and mad. Any of our children do have that right to know their father's background," our evening pot of coffee spills out on the kitchen table when my indignant wife slams down the pot, "and if you're planning to say no, just don't!"

"I would not think of it, dear, at least not now, but there is time."

"Oh no, there isn't unless eight months is enough." She stood with her hands on her hips, challenging me.

For a few moments I sat staring at her, carefully repeating her words in my head until realizing her meaning. We hugged and kissed and cried together.

I continued to use the name the Union had bestowed upon me until that idiot of a Lieutenant took me to be inducted and gave me the name of Herrington Hird, putting an "aitch" where he thought I was too stupid to pronounce properly.

From that time on I was obliged to use it for identification purposes. So now I had three authorized aliases. Nothing was done, to pursue this matter by me until my wife got on the trail seventeen years later. The attorney got interested when my wife produced the statement that was refused him and he took it upon himself to correspond to the Swiss Police departments to satisfy his curiosity. The replies he received were negative. They definitely stated that had an abandonment of that nature taken place in Berne, it could not possibly have happened without their having knowledge of it and for a very small sum they would place an advertisement in all of the Canton's villages and communes newspapers for a number of times to help in our quest. Because the news of an abandoned boy in Paris was in our hands and our purpose was to confirm or refute the Dover Police report regarding the child's supposed abandonment in the Switzerland of Europe, referenced thereof, we agreed.

Furthermore, the statement my wife received had a line in it that was omitted on the original statement I had to wait three days to obtain so long ago. Given to me was the omission that began with: "April 21st, 1904, 10:25A.M.—P.C. Mount reports." The omission of that line was important to me and the Dover Police because he, P.C. (Police Constable) Mount was still on the Police force and we Union boys knew many of the policemen because of their providing Minstrel shows. This policeman in particular was conspicuous by his ruddy complexion. It was obviously omitted Why? Because then I could ask him more questions than he would care to answer. Could he surely recall the Spanish-speaking waif in the expensive London tailored sailor suit with all that French paper money sewn in the peacoat's lining?

Later, another letter came from the new Master of the Dover Union stating that he had become curious when he discovered this unusual entry in the records so he decided to contact his predecessor regarding it. The reply he got was to the effect that he (the predecessor) remembered my coming to the Union thirty-one years before; that I had come from Switzerland with a note in my hand.

"That man is now thirty years older, but still a rotten treacherous man who had the power over all those poor people," gasped Josie, "and he's still one, just like that psychotic doctor. If I had my wish granted, I would wish for all those bed-wetters to give him a circumcision all the way up…" Josie swiped her eyes with the back of her hands.

"I remember, he was a father of two children, if they are still living, God help them. Apparently his conscience is not troubled or he is scared despite that the news of the "Lost Waif" did not reach England's presses. Which of itself is highly suspicious of nepotism. Would you agree?

"Conspiracy is on the tip of my tongue but it leaves us with still so many unanswered questions."

"I was informed by two old inmates that many foreign speaking people were brought in to question me."

"And so conveniently, no one spoke Spanish! My God, things get worse, not better. Harry, whoever you are you're too hot to be told."

My memory stirred in recalling why I had to live in the Infirmary without being sick and of that Angel who prayed for all of us paupers.

The attorney advised me to declare my illegal entry to the Immigration Department with the advice that there is no proof of nationality in my case and because a self-supporting family would be broken, he doubted that deportation proceedings would be taken.

That was done with much trepidation on my part and followed by an order giving me ninety days' notice to clear all personal matters; then to appear at Ellis Island for questioning. The Inspector at the first interview, on seeing and reading the contradictory affidavits could come to no conclusion as to disposing of my case. He was mystified as to how a person could be placed in such a predicament? When he was given all the details it used up all the time until the ferry had to leave.

He was very understanding. When, as we parted, he said, "I do not know to whom I may be talking." He wanted to shake my hand. I obliged.

A month later I was again summoned to appear at the Immigration Department on Ellis Island to be questioned or better, to be told who I was by another Inspector. At the time, I believe the feeling within me was the same as on many other occasions. I prepared myself to accept verbal abuse from where or from whom it came without retaliation, so as not to ruin my chances of remaining in a country where there was opportunity for success without having to wait for one's father to die to inherit his job; such as working on the English railroad. It is unforgettable to experience being without a father yet with political pull instead, I got a job mixing concrete by hand.

I was thinking these thoughts especially when this Inspector at the British booth told me, "You are probably an abandoned illegitimate."

As much as I felt like retorting in reply I held my tongue. He was so sure of himself when he said it or was he trying to provoke me into becoming hostile in some way, in order to keep his country full of pure-breeds like himself? But that did not make him any more of a man. During my travels, remarks of that nature had come in the form of hints but this person used his position and authority to insult. Then after listening to me explain the predicament I was in, he had a change of attitude. Tears crept into the eyes of his lovely secretary, evidently a woman with feeling and perhaps a mother.

Confronted with conditions of this nature to help me overcome, brings to my mind two famous quotes: "Judge not that ye also may not be judged," and "An atom of authority in the hands of a fool is a dangerous weapon." Regardless, this idiot was going to do his job. After his passing remarks he took me downstairs for the mug shot and fingerprinting. It seemed that he was about to put me in a cell at the time when the ferry was leaving. My being detained delayed its departure. So, thank heaven, we parted, never to meet again.

Following that episode I was not requested to appear again for a while because there were many loose threads to be joined. That required time for different departments to straighten my affairs. I received each month a notice granting me a thirty-days extension for the next three years. Then an order came early in the year for me to get a passport from the British Consulate, in order to leave the country and return legally.

On the day of receiving that notice I went to the British Consul with the affidavits issued by the different departments in England, along with my naval service discharge. I promptly obeyed the order in the hope that it would not be long now to become an American citizen.

It was a rainy Friday afternoon when I went alone because my wife was not feeling well. We were working on creating our son, James, at this time. I entered the office to be confronted by a young lady, sitting behind a counter that was as high as the useless things on my chest. It could have served as a barricade to those in that room for their protection—in the event that all applicants are favoured with the lies and conflicting statements that I had received from those worthy British officials.

On orders from Ellis Island I am now to use the name of Mornington Heard, as such a request was made for a passport in that name. But I had to produce a birth certificate. The official affidavits were insufficient unless supported by a statement from a mid-wife in lieu of the birth certificate or from a person who had known me from the time of my birth. Such statements were impossible to obtain. Not wishing to offend this person, I asked what I could do to carry out this order. She consulted a young male who gave her the statement to relay to me, that If I could produce a statement that would give me some idea as to who I was, then he would consider the issuance of a passport.

I raised the question, asking him, "In the event you do not like the idea of who I am, would you still comply?" A shrug of his shoulders and a sarcastic chuckle was his answer.

I left the British Consulate, returning to my wife, to protect myself against doing anything hasty. I had carried with me my wife's researched newspaper copies of incidents comparable to my having been disposed of at that time; such as the Waif on the High Seas.

First came an item from the English Daily Graphic, Paris edition, dated April 14th, 1904, with the caption Lost Waif. It bore the picture of the boy referred to as a chubby little fellow expensively dressed in English clothes and could not speak English. He had in his pockets a five-franc note and a slip of paper bearing the name Edward Owen but on his kerchief were the initials R de B. This information came from Le Petit Parisien, but nowhere in any of the other newspapers does it mention the money or the name.

Then came the news item from the New York Herald, Paris edition that reads with the caption: Infant Son of President Barrios Found. According to Le Petit Parisien, an extraordinary and mysterious destiny has presided over the fate of the little son of Señor Rene de Barrios, the unfortunate President of Guatemala who was assassinated two years ago. (Actually it was six years ago, on February 8th, 1898).

An abandoned child was found two weeks ago on the steps of the Madelaine Church. As the little boy's clothes bore the marks of a London clothier and he did not understand French, it was believed that he belonged to English parents. The British Embassy had him placed with an Irish nurse at the English Hospital in Levallois-Perret.

The picture of the boy was published in a number of papers and the child having been recognized by his former nurse who was in London, as the lost son of President de Barrios. The French Police were informed and the child had been taken to London. It is known that President de Barrios had an infant son at (or around) the time of his death, of whom traces had been lost and his wife could give no information as she had been in an insane asylum ever since her husband's assassination.

After these two items were read by that consulate person, he came up with the reply, "Your name does not appear," meaning of course, that the two names of Heard, did not appear in the papers. To that, I reminded him that it could not possibly be, if these names were pinned onto me after my arrival into England.

He then took this material to a superior who after reading it expressed the desire to have a copy of them. I then told him that I would take them downstairs and have photo-stats made at my expense, providing he would see that they were hung in the British Museum.

His reply to that was, "I do not like the idea of your leaving this room with those papers without my having a copy."

So I suggested that he give them to a typist in the room. Turning to the clock then towards me he stated that it was one-thirty and the office closes at four and the papers should be left with him.

Here was a person, a representative of a country, Great Britain, who would not trust me with my own property yet I was called upon to trust him. His country had deliberately supplied me with lies regarding my antecedents, in order to cover up its tracks as the perpetrator of the crime of hiring a paid assassin to kill my father, whom I honestly believe and for every good reason, was my father. My gentle Josie was working overtime on her research. God bless her.

Regarding the statement that the Waif's mother was in an insane asylum, is another complete fabrication, because a year prior to my abandonment she was living in New York City. This was not mentioned. Why? Possibly it would be for the purpose of discrediting the reporters of the New York Herald? False reports were conveniently and easily being issued because there were no direct cables from Guatemala to the United States to prove it. This is a triviality, but the British owned and operated the major presses in this Spanish speaking country and press releases had to go through their embassy. Could it be that England was the gatekeeper for news crossing borders?

However, a female typist was assigned to make copies of the material in my possession by means of a typewriter. She wore a decided look of distain as she passed me to accomplish this task. It tickled me no end, to think that I had the power to make him succumb to my wish. By way of acknowledgement for the look that I was given, I bowed low with a long sweep of my arm, holding my hat in my hand.

While this operation was in progress the consul told me that he would not issue a passport because I was not a British subject. This suited me to no end, if he would put it in writing. He refused to do so instead he said that he would call Ellis Island to that effect.

That gave me the opportunity to become insulting, to a point where a disturbance could be made to bring about my arrest, when I replied, "I do not trust the word of an Englishman."

He did not reply with words but judging by his expression and the extreme brilliance of colour that came to his fair complexion, it became obvious that had he had his wish I would soon go the way of my father, the President. To bring that portion of the proceedings to an end, the first male I spoke to, was authorized to tell my wife who waited in the outer office that a traveler's passport back to England would be issued at half-price because of my wartime service. Would she like to make the payment now?

"Of course not! You're crazy if you think my husband will fall for that nasty trick

The first time to your country almost killed him. What will it be this time? The Tower of London or some dungeon or just throw him overboard?"

I smothered my grin, admiring that lovely voice drifting through this closed door. I was reminded that there may be insufficient time to complete the work before the closing hour.

In return I reminded him, "You say I am not a British subject yet I have done many hours overtime during the war for his Majesty's service, so it should not hurt you, Sir, to do a little overtime, as you are a servant of the Royal Crown."

He had the copies that he so desired then we left. Four days later we received a letter from the British consulate dated ironically, exactly forty-one years to the day after the assassination of President General José Maria Reyna Barrios by a British subject on February 8th, 1939, that read:

Sir'

With reference to your recent visit to this Consulate-General, I have considered your position and feel that nothing could be gained by my referring your case to the Foreign Office, since you have already attempted unsuccessfully to obtain verification of your claim to British nationality from both, the Home Office and the Registrar General of Births, Deaths and Marriages.

It is possible that, in view of your long residence in Great Britain and of your period of service in the War, exceptional arrangements might be made to enable you to return to England if you so desired; but it is most unlikely that I should be authorized to grant you a passport for any other purpose. In any event a passport unsupported by documentary evidence of your place and date of birth would be of little use to you, since I understand that, even though eligible for preferential treatment as the husband of an American citizen, you will still have to be allotted a quota number and that the quota is based on the place of birth of the applicant; It would therefore be impossible for you to obtain a visa under the normal procedure.

In the circumstances I would recommend you to communicate to the American Consul-General at Montreal, making a complete statement of your position and asking whether it would be possible for you to apply for a visa on an affidavit, owing to your inability to obtain a national passport. I am enclosing for your convenience a copy of this letter, which you may submit to the American Consul-General at the same time as proof of the fact that you were unable to establish a claim to British nationality.

I am,
Sir,
Your obedient Servant,

C.E. Kenball
H.M.B.Consul
For H.M.B. Consul-General.

This document is so full of holes; reminiscent of the other departments that are supposed to be servants of the populace. They are even willing to make an exception in my case by stating that a passport is impossible to issue unless it is for me to return to England without being a British subject. Statements made like this tend to show positions of that kind are not given on the merit system. Being found as an abandoned kid; taken to that country from another country; presumed to be of that nationality yet not speaking a word of English; detained in their orphanage for eleven years; served in its defense; only now to have another person trample me into the ground!

Let it be known that at no time did I ever try to claim England as my country. On the contrary, it has been my purpose to discredit them—claims made by them, that I was ever presumed to be British.

Had that been the case, I would have not jumped ship in order to stay here and now I would certainly not leave my wife behind, who having this knowledge of my upbringing, would definitely have no desire to go there. Her welfare was not, and that of our two young daughters, taken under consideration. That clearly demonstrated their desire to get hold of me once more. The back door was left open so I just went through it, to the country that was mentioned a number of times by my Schoolmaster, as the closest to being self supporting and powerful. To live with an attractive and intelligent woman who knew and liked who she was. To become a lost waif no more.

The monthly notices were still coming each month; notifying me that another thirty day extension had been granted. These continued to come until September of that year when on the eighth day of that month a letter came from Ellis Island telling me to report at a specified time on that day.

When the word got around that I had come, I was ordered to appear in a room where ten Inspectors had assembled with the purpose of offering a suggestion to put an end to the dilemma I had created. A discussion of my case had been held with the result that if I would leave the country to go to Canada at my own expense with a letter to guarantee my return, would I consent and how soon?

My hesitation was made evident as I did not immediately respond. Ten pairs of eyes bore into me.

"What is the matter?" One voice echoed in the silent room.

"Sir, I have had too many years spent with lies. Before, I just had myself to care for. My circumstance is changed."

"I see your point, Mr. Heard. You're afraid for your family, is that it?"

"Precisely, Sir."

"What if we supply security to you and your family? We need witnesses to see that you are coming through Canada to apply for U. S. citizenship. A formality but it satisfies all the rules," he laughed, "besides, all these agents and I spent a lot of time looking at your case. Don't disappoint us. Your case is one in a rare million and I'm itching for those Brits to kick up a fuss. Whoever you are they're keeping it secret from the looks of things. But understand, Mr. Heard, if you do agree, you'll have to go now."

"Sir?"

"You're not the only one who doesn't trust them. I'll have you get going before they have time to know you're gone and they can't do a damned thing about it. Understand me?"

I did not attempt to hide my grin, "Mostly assuredly, Sir, and I'm much obliged to all of you gentlemen."

Hands came out to shake mine. Coming from different voices, "Good luck, Mr. Whoever you are?"

"Better go home and tell your wife."

"Good luck, pal, we'll be here waiting for you."

On those terms I agreed to go on the next train, this night. I was informed, that if I am detained by the Canadian Customs Officers, I should demand to make a telephone call to the American Consul-General. Also, the American officers at the border would be notified of my coming, as a further safe guard.

The train left at midnight, arriving in Montreal in the morning but I was held for a short time only to explain my mission and although I was not able to produce a passport I was treated as a British subject and allowed to go.

The meeting with the American Consul-General was very pleasant. He was a true representative of democracy. He called me into his office for the purpose of explaining in detail, the cause for my being in this predicament that was so confusing to him and his staff. He listened intently as I gave the reasons for the British Consul making such a ridiculous statement and telling him that I was the one abandoned in Paris, was the reason for their taking me to England. After listening to me without interruption, he wrote out a visa this way:

> NAME:Errington Herd, Herrington Hird, Mornington Heard
> FATHER'S NAME: unknown,
> MOTHER'S BIRTHPLACE: unknown,
> NATIONALITY: none.

Armed with this unusual visa, I could now board the train for Canada, to re-enter the country that gave me my first citizenship. Nothing of consequence happened to me on my train ride to Canada or back. But an occurrence of a curious nature did take place. I paid no attention to the pair of gents occupying seats across the aisle. They got off the train when I did. Hours later, when I am waiting to board at the deserted train depot I notice these two men again who, in turn, also notice two other well dressed gentlemen moving on the shadowy outside platform. The first pair go to the second pair who are moving farther back on the platform when seeing their company advancing toward them. There is a brief exchange of words. I hear their hushed tones to recognize the mixture of Yankee and British accents. One of my train-travelers swiftly produces a gun, jammed to the Brit's waist close to him. Then they are gone! I am wondering if I imagined all this as the travelers walk past me with one winking at me and the other one giving me a bare imperceptible nod.

However coincidental, it was not long after our visit to the British Consul that a news item appeared in the papers-that all the records of a Police Station in Paris had been stolen. For more coincidence, with all the police stations within this huge metropolis, the theft happened at the one where Froggie was on file.

Josie was still pursuing all the angles for possible information but the chief source would not cooperate, that was Le Petit Parisien. That paper, when contacted by letter, stated that the items she requested were in their archives and could not be given without the consent of the government.

She also made a trip to Washington, DC, to see if there was information of value in the Library of Congress. She found that the whole bound volume of the London Daily Graphic for the month of April (1904) had been removed. The Head Librarian was shocked.

It appears that foreign consulates work fast but it does not mean they are smarter than my wife, when it comes to seeking information on topics making news, because she is confident that American reporters contact others to compare notes and that makes it all the easier for our researching.

Now, it is time to concentrate on the report of Señora Reyna de Barrios abandoning her daughter in the same place, believe it or not.

13

Lost Waif Is a Girl

The picture and the description of the *Lost Child* showed it was a boy yet an item in the New Orleans Times Picayune reported that Mrs. Reyna de Barrios abandoned her daughter on the steps of the Madelaine. This paper may or may not have had good reasons for publishing this but the thought comes to my mind that this false information was inserted for propaganda purposes. It was in this city that Señora Reyna de Barrios lived as a girl. Growing up, her name was Lilly or Algerie Bates or Benton and because of her beauty, fair complexion with blue eyes, she was called Lily, after the flower.

It is true that a girl was placed in a convent in London, given the name of Consuelo de Barrios, who was brought there by a person from the office of the Guatemalan Minister. It is known that Mrs. Reyna de Barrios went to the convent to visit this child, but involuntarily.

According to the Mother Superior, Mrs. Reyna de Barrios, when visiting the convent, was always accompanied by a nurse because this supposed mother always came drugged to a stupefacient degree and at no time did she show any affection for this girl. Also, she (Consuelo), bore no resemblance, whatsoever, to either the late President or the lady who came to the Convent.

The Mother Superior had no contacts with the outside world, such as reading newspapers, so it was a simple matter to substitute a girl for the boy who had so many names, such as Rene de Barrios, Edward Owen, and Edward Britton, according to the Vice-Consul in New York.

Yet another report stated that the boy was taken *to* his mother, Mrs. Brittain. This last name came from the Metropolitan Police in London after Mrs. Turner (the boy's nanny) positively identified the child as the son of the assassinated President of Guatemala. Then she vanished and was never seen again.

Therefore, cannot it be justifiably assumed that Mornington Heard and Errington Herd, found in similar suits (expensively tailored sailor outfits with caps and little navy pea-coats) and also, neither one was speaking English, and both were reported to be abandoned within that same short period in time are not one and the same as the publicized child? Incidentally, I had to wear that sailor suit for a year of Sundays, until the seams threatened to split apart but I could have boasted, if I so desired, of being the richest dressed pauper in the institution only no other Union inmate was speaking Spanish. One thing is certain, I will not lay claim to being Consuelo.

Consuela was a sick girl the whole time of *eleven* years she spent in the convent, suffering from asthma and bronchitis. Was she allergic to England's climate? At the end of that time, in the month of February 1915, she was (reported) to have been sent to Guatemala to live but four years later she then died in New Orleans. The sad news of her death was publicized in order to bring to the attention of the readers that she, as a little girl, had been abandoned in Paris. But this was the only paper that carried this untruth. So, here is the end for one of three Lost Waifs.

14

The Father of the Lost Waif

There is no reason to doubt the identity of the *Lost Waif* as that of the assassinated President of Guatemala that was brought to light by Le Petit Parisien and the New York Herald, also including the slightly twisted version of the London Daily Graphic.

The President of Guatemala was born in 1854, on Christmas Eve. He was but five years old when a part of his country was handed over to the British in an agreement. In return, roads and railways would be built, accompanied with a payment of a certain amount of money for a designated amount of territory. More than the specified amount of land was taken and later was to become known as British Honduras. The full payment in money was not made and as far as is known today, the roads were not built.

José had an uncle, Justo Rufino Barrios, who was of partial Indian ancestry that automatically made him a kind of outcast with the white Europeans who were prospering in this rich land.

For example, while attending school Justo went to the home of one classmate to borrow a book to help with his education. When he called at the house he was led to understand that on no account must he enter. This incident so infuriated him that he made a vow. He would some day be president and to that direction he worked hard enough to fulfill this promise. Achieving his goal, he then appointed his nephew, Colonel José Maria Reyna Barrios to the position of Consul in Hamburg, Germany. José was well received that eventually led to that country getting the lion's share of the commerce from Guatemala, with England getting but six per cent.

In 1885, President Justo Rufino Barrios was killed in a questionable battle with el Salvador. It was questionable because of certain factors. Present Justo Barrios did not want war with his neighbor, el Salvador, as they and the other surrounding countries knew they needed each other for their survival and protection. Justo sent word to meet privately with the other country's leader to talk for working out their problems. Justo sent word on ahead to alert his colleague that he was on his way for their conference. But just across the border Guatemala's leader meets with his death. Only a few of his soldiers are with him. It is then learned that the message sent from Guatemala was not the same message received in el Salvador. Of the small unit of men traveling horseback, only Justo is shot dead from a sniper's rifle. This ends the supposed battle with el Salvador also horrified with this outcome. Both countries sadly mourn this man's death. He had led Guatemala out of its dark times into a more stable land. The harm was done although it was well known that the British had control over both countries' network of communications. No news passed through the embassies unless the gatekeepers sanctioned it. Could this perhaps be why not a word of a president's son is ever mentioned in any Spanish newspaper?

One year before Justo's murder, José returned from Germany for a visit to New York City where he later attended a social gathering of well-to-do people. In the group was a very beautiful girl; golden hair, blue eyed, and light complexion, who was attending school and living with her uncle and his family Although she was born in Alabama, she attended a convent in New Orleans, where she resided. She was much younger than José, but that did not deter him from wooing her to eventually become his wife. The honeymoon was to be spent touring Europe before returning to his own country, Guatemala.

Manuel Barillas succeeded Justo Rufino Barrios in the presidency. His term of office ended in 1892. During the years that Barillas held power, he spent a large fortune on his mistress, an American girl, to the extent that after his murder in Mexico and his creditors had been paid which left his estate in cash, the sum of fifty-two dollars five cents.

While holding this position, Barillas appointed José Maria Reyna de Barrios to the post of Minister of War. Following this office, the General Assembly made José Division General of the Army. This was in recognition of his service in the battle with el Salvador and before this, when at the age of fifteen José led a group of volunteers to fight against the country's tyranny.

In 1892 José was made President for a six-year term of office that would end in March of 1898. He had the distinction of being the first President to be elected by popular vote. His uncle, Justo Barrios had the distinction of coming to the presidency when his predecessor turned the office over to him as he retired. For the dozen years in power Justo is credited with being known as the Reformer. His gravesite is still a national shrine at the General Cemetery in Guatemala City.

A few months before José's term of office was to end, the government appointed him to succeed himself as their President. This undoubtedly proved his popularity among the people although there were many statements issued to the contrary after his death that was brought about by an assassin's bullet at eight o'clock on the eighth day of February on Eighth Street, Guatemala City, in the year of 1898.

The assassin was immediately shot by the President's guards. He was identified as one who had been in the country only about three weeks and had been offered the sum of one hundred thousand dollars to perpetuate this crime.

He was a young man of twenty-three years and a British subject who was reported to be a naturalized Swiss. This hired killer who originally came from the Switzerland of the Eastern Hemisphere, ironically ends his days in the Switzerland of the Western Hemisphere.

From that alone, one can deduce why England issued so many bungling and conflicting statements regarding the *Lost Waif*. A major cover up! How many Brits were concealing their wrong doings and crimes? Who was to pay out that bundle of money? Where and how did I fit into their scheme? What really happened to my mother? There is no one in this world having a better right than me to claim these truths. Regardless of what statements are issued to the contrary, it would be very difficult to prove their veracity when men in power gain special privileges not afforded to most others

Turning back to the time following this criminal act, President José Barrios was succeeded by the First Vice-President; as there were two elected Vice-Presidents, Señor Morales, who held this position for only six months. Then his demise occurs. Rumors floated that Morales' death was caused by Señor Cabrera, the Second Vice-President and that he also caused the murder in Mexico of Barillas There was evidence of close ties existing between Morales and José Barrios. Cabrera's rule was vengeful and extraordinarily cruel. He formed his own private army with soldiers-of fortune world wide, to protect himself against his own countrymen. This is one of the country's few Presidents who was non-military but raised the definition of "horror" to another torturous dimension.

Many people who supported José fled the country, fearing their outcome with President Cabrera. Among them was José's widow who, it is known, gave birth to a posthumous child in Guatemala City. Prior to his death José was known to be worth inestimable millions but when his estate was settled the news given to the American newspapers was that he also left but fifty-two dollars, five cents. Coincidentally again, this is the exact amount left after President Barillas' death.

After President Morales' death, the next to hold that position was José's lawyer, (Second Vice-President Cabrera) who had full charge of all Barrios' personal assets. This man was a supposed friend, because José gave him a start when he was struggling in his law practice. He proved to be a psychotic tyrant of the worst kind

Josie was unrelenting in her search for the truths. She admitted her ignorance of all the Central American countries due to disinterest because she was trained to believe that these countries carried on major bloodshed as a daily habit. Not until dealing into my past did so many other doors came to light.

An observation my dear wife made one day, "You know, I think you're a Joseph."

"What?"

"A Joseph."

"Why?"

"That news item with you being brought to Victoria Station in London and that woman we can't find anymore. I forget her name just now but your Nanny?"

"Mrs Turner said, "That's my little Rene, not Joseph, dear."

"Yes, but listen. Your father dies in February and you're born in early June that year. What would be the best honor for a grieving mother to give her son? His father's name. And since she knows she won't be having more of his children she does this. And if your nursemaid nickname's you, R-e-n-e, for Reyna Barrios. Besides, my parents hoped for a boy when I came along. They were running out of baby time so I was named Josephine or Joseph if I was a boy."

"I am much obliged to them, dear." He touched her swollen stomach. Do you have a name picked out for this one?"

"Not yet but I'm hoping for a boy this time. Lorraine and Bunny are healthy little stinkers but a "tyke" as you would say, would round out our brood. Now let me go, Joe, so I can get food on the table."

From that day forward my wife has called me Joe. Our son was born on Thanksgiving Day that year. We call him James. I am truly happy. I promised Josie not to ruin her holidays anymore than I have. Lorraine (Rainbow) is our July fourth firecracker and Esther (Bunny) arrived on Easter Sunday.

15

The Mother of the Lost Waif

It has been three evenings since Josie and I could sit down to discuss the progress of her latest research. Our three children are tucked in their respective beds. Our Brooklyn apartment building is located on 711 Vernon Avenue. I have to now share my wife with Western Union Telegraph Company, but I mind not in the least. My brood is all mine in her absence and when I have to answer an emergency call to repair a broken water pipe or drain water from a steam radiator, they come with me or temporarily stay with Helen, our cook, or Margaret, our housekeeper. Lo and behold, how I cannot stop grinning whenever I mention these employees. One wonders how an apartment building superintendent, not even a glorified one, makes his pelf? By honest and gratifying means, I assure you. Having also spent time in an orphanage, Josie and I paid a visit upon a local one. The women had not been blessed with beauty or brains but they were unwanted adults. During weekdays they shared a bedroom with us and returned to the orphanage for weekends and holidays. The small stipends for housing these social cast-offs went back to them as wages, but this part of the arrangement was kept amongst us, not their Supervisor. As the super's seven room-suite was gratis, besides a small monthly wage, we could share our wealth and still be comfortable. We became a family of four adults and three children that lasted a long time.

"Pour the coffee and I'll get the file," Josie hurried towards our bedroom.

Nothing more than a carton that canned food goods is packaged is the case file. The carton could hold another three inches of stacked papers but I still would call this amount of collected letters and documents a sizable amount and continually thickening. It has become a ritual to sit in the kitchen late at night, discussing "the case."

"How do you ever know where to put each paper?"

"Simple, dear, by date. I even cross-index by countries. See? E, F, G and U. So if you're looking for a paper from…"

"Dover," I supplied.

"Find big folder E, for England, and smaller sub folder D inside, thumb through the papers for the approximate date you think you want and then it's here." Josie took the cigarette I rolled for her from the Bugler can. She in turn poured a bit of condensed milk into my coffee. We could anticipate each one's habits and wants so often.

I saw her frown. "What is the matter?"

"First there was nothing to go by for answers, now there's so much that it's too much. It's too confusing. We've been over these newspaper articles time and again and I am convinced that your mother is not your mother in New Orleans but she is your mother in London and Guatemala. I must be too dense to figure this out, but things are really tangled up. I'm sorry dear, I know how much you want to find her, dead or alive."

I laughed because I had been thinking similar thoughts. "Do not feel sorry, Josie. I believe there were two Madams Barrios and both are gone."

"Really?" She crushed out her cigarette. "I don't like how the reporters describe her. There are too many changes in her behavior and what she tells the reporters. It's like they described different females at different times. Why do you think so?"

"Attitudes, like you say but also eyes. One has blue eyes, the other brown."

"What?"

"My eyes are blue. If my father was Spanish with brown eyes who mated with the brown eyed mother, would I have this colour eyes?"

"How did I miss that?"

"Because you were not looking for the obvious. This is why I like the reporters who helped me sort out my mother by her eyes. She was the one I hugged good-bye at Victoria Station."

"To think I was afraid of hurting you with my opinion." Taking a sip of steaming coffee, "Go on, talk."

I began. "At the time the boy was found on the steps of the Madelaine in Paris, a statement was put out by their press, that the mother of the boy had been in an insane asylum since the death of her husband. This can be proven to be erroneous because immediately following the tragedy that befell her, she fled from Guatemala just like many who were staunch supporters of the Barrios family."

"Political exiles?" She rolled two cigarettes.

"Yes, dear, but even more than that. Cabrera indiscriminately seized so much land and wealth from anyone that he wanted. Total families were destroyed all because he wanted to be the President. And he needed a constant supply of money to support his private army in order to stay the President."

"Let's talk about your mothers. This means I better re-examine all the files on Algerie de Barrios and see where blue eyes is when brown eyes is not." Josie picks up the papers she placed on top of the carton that have not been filed as yet. "For instance, we know that in 1901 she takes up residence in New York City and two years later she is arrested in Manhattan, mostly for her strange behavior. She hires a cab, horse drawn of course, to take her to the Waldorf Astoria Hotel with the intention of visiting the Guatemalan Minister whom she knows is staying there. Gee, I'd like to know why she went to him? Social or business?"

"We will never know, dear."

"Anyway, she arrives but doesn't get out of the cab. She tells the cabbie to drive her around for a while before asking him to go back to the Hotel again. This procedure happens again before the cabbie calls a policeman and explains to him the strange antics of his fare, who has no fare money. She appears frightened, weak and drugged by the looks in her pale *blue* eyes, these men say. Because Blue Eyes has no money, so she is locked up overnight at the local precinct and to appear before a Magistrate in the morning. Probably for vagrancy charges." Josie stops to refill her coffee.

I lean across the table to where she put down the newspaper clipping. "According to the Matron at the Police Station, she confided in her, a most remarkable story of events. Unfortunately, if that was publicized there are no traces of it to be found but this much is known, when she appeared before the Magistrate's bench, she had no shoes, even at the time of her arrest. However, two men came to the trial, made restitution in her behalf and she was then put in the custody of these supposed *benefactors*. (I could visualize what this frightened woman, my poor mother, felt).

"One incident she did mention when asked the reason for being barefooted, she cried that she had been kept under guard in the Pierrepont Hotel and she had evaded her captors. The two men denied her story, convincing the court that the president's widow was not well because of her mentality due to medications and alcohol. The younger of the two men claimed to be her nephew while the other was a British friend. She was their prisoner."

Josie's eyes fluttered. They were wet. "Oh God, Joe. All this was a cover up for greed. We still don't know the whole story yet but we know it covers three continents, so there has to be more than just a few persons in on it." Her graceful hand slipped into mine.

"Assuming she was being drugged to keep her subdued, where am I?"

"I don't know? Paris, like the newspaper said?"

"How did I get there? I am small and could pass for younger than a boy of six in April of 1904.. And Mrs. Turner? My nursemaid or nanny is in London. If she knows me well, than do you not think that there is a possibility my mother was hiding me with her? But if I am speaking Spanish, than it is likely that my mother would hire someone who could communicate with me?"

"I haven't thought of it, but you're right."

I had given much thought to this issue. I now verbalized it. "But I do not have any suggestion as to how I got to the Church to be found there. I surely did not make that journey alone. Someone else brought me, not my mother. I keep wondering about the name on the paper I have in my pocket. Edward Owen. Nevertheless, Mrs. Turner had to be eliminated if just for speaking Spanish. She could and almost did ruin all the many planned lies. Why did I not leave that depot with my mother after being found?"

The next report that I perused concerned my mother that appeared in Le Petit Parisien a year later, when she appeared at the Victoria Station, awaiting the arrival of the *Lost Waif*. When she arrived, there was an Inspector from the London Police Department standing with two women. One woman was beautiful and was conversing gaily. The other was described as a tough, middle class boarding house keeper. The younger one was also typed as an adventuress.

The correspondent for the French paper was present and knew the Inspector by sight as he sat beside Mrs. de Barrios, asking her the reason for abandoning her son. She confessed to doing it but in the hope that some well-to-do people would find him first and care for him.

While this was taking place, the boy's nurse appeared, who emphatically said that upon seeing the picture of the *Lost Waif* in the newspaper, she immediately got in touch with the London Metropolitan Police and said that it definitely was her little Rene (nickname), meaning Reyna de Barrios but the British Consul discredited her story. This woman who had taken care of Rene for a year, was Mrs. Turner. After that day, this woman vanished from London.

The train carrying the *Lost Waif* arrived. Mrs. Turner and the real mother, together, ran the full length of the train in the hope that they would be the first to get to him but that was not to be. He was on the platform when they returned.

The mother went down on her knees, hugging and showering kisses on him as they cried but this heart-rendering scene was soon ended by the Inspector taking the boy from his mother, also taking with him, Mrs. Turner. The two women described earlier and Mrs. de Barrios were left on the station.

Years later, this Scotland Yard Detective (the Inspector) wrote his memoirs. Often have I wondered what his version of that episode was, knowing that he was consorting with two opportunists before the genuine persons appeared. He did not take the mother, the one who had admitted leaving the child, no, because the many names that were bestowed on him could not possibly stick with her being on the scene. The trail had to be covered and Mrs. Turner knew the real waif and his mother. Without doubt, she would have to be eliminated.

This happened on the twenty-eighth day of April, 1904, exactly two weeks after finding the boy, so does one have to assume that the records on Mornington Heard are pertaining to an entirely different person because the dates printed in the newspapers are one week apart? No one in his right mind would dare question the integrity or efficiency of the Official persons who have made all these conflicting statements that have gone to press, except if everyone is serving in the Marines.

Is it not to be wondered if this boy's mother was persecuted to this extent that her behaviour on the railroad station, after her child was taken from her, showed clearly that she was resigned to her fate? What could the motive be on the part of the authorities to render such treatment? Believe it or not, it was out of respect.

She was both respected and feared because of her knowledge of International Politics. In 1915 she died in England after spending her last eleven years being forcibly drugged and made to visit a sick girl in a convent who was unrelated in order to support the false story given to the newspapers.

This was not made public property but when some information comes from the Mother Superior of a convent, it has no place in the files, to be defiled by the lies from police and consuls. She has blessed us with the first truthful statement without question; to inform us of the continued persecution of a childless Mother. As these were conflicting stories about her child, so also was there one about her when an imposter was placed in the Alms House in New Orleans-being the mother of Consuelo. The web of deceit was so thick with treachery, that it was not known until much later how many Barrios family members were persecuted or murdered.

16

Lost Waif, American Version

There was no letting up on the part of my wife to get all the material pertaining to this strange incident of mine. But the time had come however, when she could no longer extract any more untruths from the British authorities. It was due to the problem involving all the people in that country in another war (WWII) caused by the actions of a maniac in another country, Germany. As yet, America was not a participant. The New York City Library was not affected and its doors were still open to this daily visitor with one purpose in her mind.

Day after day, she would spend hours scouring all the American papers made available to her, covering the period from the turn of the century. This continued for many months. Even the New York Herald did not have news of the abandoned child. It was then, that she decided to visit the Library of Congress, in the hope of getting a larger assortment from which to choose. The selection was no better in Washington, D C so she returned home, frustrated but not defeated. Then another avenue opened. What better way is there to obtain what she sought than to write to the newspapers?

The paper, New York Herald, admitted to not providing coverage of the news requested (no reason given) but referred her to the New Orleans Times Picyune. The story that appeared in that paper was pertaining to the death of the girl who was raised in the British Convent, with the caption, *DEATH WRITES FINAL CHAPTER IN TRAGEDY OF GUATEMALA. Consuela Reyna Barrios, The Little Lady of Sorrow, posthumous child of murdered President Barrios, finds last resting place in New Orleans.*

This article goes on to state that when this girl, supposed Barrios' daughter, was born, she was raised by President Estrada Cabrera who by way of effecting importance (or covering his tracks), attached the title of Godfather of Consuelo to himself.

It was evident that this newspaper was naïve, gullible or with intent to spread misleading propaganda. When my wife questioned the source of the story, she learned that all press releases from and to other countries or continents, always passed through embassies, especially with the consent from the consulates' offices.

This same paper stated that Mrs. Reyna Barrios abandoned her daughter on the steps of the Madelaine in Paris. That was one year after the boy (me) had been found in the very same place. Then, when this girl died, this paper reported that Estrada Cabrera raised this child and sent her to England to be educated at the Convent. To add a bit more intrigue, the Convent is the same one that the blue-eyed Madam Barrios was brought to under sedation, in order to visit her brown eyed daughter, whom she did not recognize, nor did the girl recognize her supposed mother.

This unfortunate young lady, Consuela, met her death along with her twenty-first birthday. Her *devoted* Godfather, President Cabrera, most patriotically demanded the return of this convent-dweller once World War II started. He commissioned her services into the Red Cross in New Orleans, where she succumbed to an unknown ailment.

Furthermore, from another of Josie's clippings, it was also reported that on New Years Day, 1910, that this supposed mother applied for admission to the Alms House in New Orleans, at the age of thirty-three, when the fact is that the real First Lady was married two decades before. Also, this applicant was described as a tall lady with velvety *brown* eyes. Consuelo did have brown eyes. As time went on, those in charge of fabrications were becoming carelessly sloppy. The politically persecuted lady at this time in 1910 was still in England with very little chance of leaving and she was very beautiful, having *blue* eyes, of petite, regal carriage.

In these contradictory statements one can see a connection in this regard, when, at the time the train was to arrive in London, bringing the boy, there was a woman waiting, who, according to the London correspondent for Le Petit Parisien, acted the role of also being the waif's mother. She was also attractive but looked Jewish-with dark hair and *brown* eyes, wrote the reporter. Nowhere, is it reported that when the First Lady of Guatemala gave birth to whichever child, did she ever live at the home of President Estrada Cabrera. Perhaps now may be a good time to say that I have a small build and see through pale blue eyes. It may mean nothing, just coincidental, but my wife's research proves that José and Algerie were both of diminutive stature. Judging by characteristics in appearance from newspaper pictures, could Consuelo possibly be the not-delightful gift of Cabrera's and the New Orleans woman, Miss Bates? It is also known that Cabrera never ventured outside of his native land for fear of being murdered but also he could not afford to transport his private army with him if he so desired a vacation abroad. The hombre literally had no life beyond Guatemala's boundaries. But the brown-eyed actress vacationed in Guatemala, France, Switzerland, England and the United States, among other purposes.

It became evident that this woman, who had been described as an adventuress six years earlier, nevertheless was still in the game of substitution for as much gain as the perpetrator of the assassination of President Reyna Barrios.

Why would a crazed man like Cabrera allow the widow's pension to be collected by a stand-in? Since it was dubious that the man had a heart, is it realistic to surmise a payoff for *acting* services rendered?

At the time of the Victoria train station incident, this woman is very talkative to the press. I compared this with the interview that took place on the platform seated on a bench with the reporter of the French paper, by the real mother.

Talkative Brown Eyes also makes an effort to describe the assassination in detail by saying that after dinner that evening, she separated from her husband by going to her dressing room, leaving him to walk down a long curved corridor when he was shot.

Whereas, it is a known fact that José is shot *outside* the National Palace and on the grounds while walking with guards, who immediately shot the killer. She does not give the name of the one who did it, yet it was made known by the Guatemalan press.

Another press release stated that she had been receiving fifty dollars a month from the Guatemalan Government (stated the Guatemalan consul in New Orleans) but should she decide to return to that country she would receive a pension equal to her husband's salary. In this statement also, it says that she left her daughter in a hotel in Paris yet nowhere does it state that she left an address in New Orleans before applying to be taken into the Poor House.

With each newspaper clipping came a bit of truth amongst many unanswerable questions. For instance, the monthly allotment of fifty dollars would not suffice for self-support but it was sufficient in that time to support some personal habits, especially when one has her mother, alive and well, living in the vicinity. Then, would not this hidden lady be related to Consuelo, as her Grandmother?

If Brown Eyes needed money, why not return to Guatemala? She, like the assassin, had been imported, probably being of the impression that there were good times to be had at the expense of a really persecuted mother. It is too bad that she was unable to speak to the murderer, Oscar Zollinger, before venturing on such an undertaking, as acting as an imposter, influenced no doubt, by promises that were never intended to be fulfilled by Estrada Cabrera or anyone else.

Once England had mother and son interred in their facilities, Cabrera did not need Brown Eyes.

"I would like your opinion, dear," I began one evening session with the coffee cups and Bugler tobacco between us. "I have no doubt that my mother and I were being held as hostages. Mr. Cabrera obtained the presidency and just took his wealth. We could not threaten his reign but why did the British want us alive? We became two more mouths to feed in an impoverished country. Sending us back to Central America would have been akin to having us murdered."

"Darned if I know but whatever the British conspirators wanted, I do not believe they ever got it. And if Consuelo died on her twenty-first birthday, I think the same was scheduled for you but you ran off when war came."

My one visit to the British Consulate was enough to convince me not to put trust in any statement coming from that department. I recall when verbally being told that a passport would be issued at half price, then sending to me the utterly ridiculous letter to the effect that although I was not a British subject I would be issued one for that country. Had the Consulate forgotten that Canada at that time was a part of the British Empire?

This stand-in woman's life ended five years later in the boarding home of a family in New Orleans. On that fatal night, the man of that house made preparations for her funeral but later that *same* night, he suddenly died, too. This leaves an unanswered question and more. Did he know too much? Both deaths have questionable causes.

When Josie contacted this deceased man's daughter she was evasive, however, this did not deter my wife from pursuing this event. So, she placed a small advertisement in a New Orleans paper that brought a reply from an elderly man living nearby. He had seen the dead woman (Brown Eyes) a matter of a few days earlier to her death. She was sitting on the front porch of her benefactor. The informant furnished the name and address of a niece who attended to the woman until one hour before she died.

My wife contacted this person. She said she knew the woman from previous visits to her uncle's house and was told that the deceased woman was the wife to a Spanish nobleman. The widow of President Justo Rufino Barrios (José's uncle) was Francesca Aparicio Barrios and was reported to have married such a person with that kind of title. Later, he proved to be nothing more than a senator in Spain.

Moreover, there was yet another Barrios widow, who was the wife of José's brother, who was assassinated one year before José's assassination.

Giving this dead woman the benefit of the doubt, it becomes probable that if she was the widow of one Barrios member (Barrios clan was quite numerous) she definitely was not the widow of José Maria Reyna Barrios.

The death certificate reports her age as being fifty, whereas, five years before, when she went to the Poor House she was thirty-three. The newspaper states that at the time of her death she is but forty. Taking into account all the conflicting reports in the French, English and American newspapers and the many names given to the Lost Waif by the British authorities, it rather seems that the British were caught with their britches down and could not conveniently hike them up.

Either someone lacked creativity or was attempting to leave me a clue so many years ago. In perusing the city map of London, my wife discovered a specific district having a street and a road named after me. Mornington Road is near Heard Street.

Because there is a difference of only one week in the dates when the boy is taken to England and the one brought from Switzerland (who never existed), some authorities are convinced that I am not the waif. Or to put it another way, they are trying to convince my wife to that effect. Yet no one addresses the days I spent somewhere that I vaguely remember. A nice big house and a kind lady who took care of me, before I had to leave with a well dressed man. Could this kind woman be Mrs. Turner, my Nanny? Was this the week in question? That alone is their only reason for denying that I was not the waif.

There was a mistake made when I was sent to school to be taught that two and two added, come to zero. Another is that the Dover Police did not send one of its men to escort me to the Union, as was the law. So, how did I get there? I think the tall man brought me by train yet he left no calling card and later became non-existent..

If I was smart enough at that age to find my way alone, after coming from a foreign country and not being able to speak the language, I think I have enough savvy to know, that they are a bunch of "Bloody Liars."

The elderly man who answered the advertisement continued to give further help in our quest for information pertaining to the dead woman by giving the name of the undertaker. That was omitted on the death certificate. Also known is the fact that she (Brown Eyes) died three hours before the man at the same address. The file number is two behind that of the man's. After his making inquiries as to where she was buried, he went to the cemetery to find the grave. Here he was given an ultimatum, to leave or else. Still, he did not want to disappoint us so he contacted a Brother (from the religious order) who advised him not to continue his investigation.

Therein lies the American version of the Lost Waif, just as confusing and contradictory in all respects as the European side of the tale but in them, both speak of persecution to a mother, her son and another's daughter. Also, there is the double crossing of the assassin (Zollinger) and of the brown eyed adventuress. It is confusing, as it all seems. One can only ask, why? The supposed daughter, Consuelo, died at the home of her grandmother in 1915 yet the woman was in New Orleans five years before but there is no mention of her going to her mother or of any relative coming to see her in the Poor House or of her Godfather's bereavement.

One version of Mrs. Reyna Barrios was that she was married while staying at the home of her uncle, Doctor Thomas Easton, whom the American Medical Association is interested in knowing what happened to him in order to complete their files. He seemed to have been misplaced. They in turn have asked us to forward this information should we ever acquire it. The search for it took us as far back as 1889, when Dr. Easton was living on East Twelfth Street, New York. Her name is assumed to be Lillian Bates. She traveled extensively, lived in New Orleans at different times and was an actress, by trade.

Then there is the other version of a girl born in New Orleans who was orphaned in Birmingham, Alabama and had a court assigned, self-appointed guardian who was the city's District Attorney. She ran away on the northbound train to New York to escape a planned marriage, but this is another whole story. Of interest is the fact that Gertrude Benton, this runaway, wanted a singing career and disliking Gertrude, she chose Algerie Benton.

One lady had said nothing since the day the boy was brought from France, whereas, the imposter spoke about everything-all lies. My wife attained a copy of a Guatemalan document declaring duel citizenship to Algerie Reyna de Barrios before her replacement arrived on the scenes. Which one is tall? Which one is small? Which one has blue eyes? Bates or Benton? Both beautiful women spoke fluent English, French and Spanish. Both lived at different times in Guatemala City, New York City, New Orleans, London, and all over. But one had at least ten years over the other woman. Hereafter, my wife would take time to sort out and research all these details and lots more.

17

Lost Waif Writes to His Mothers

Dear Mrs. Britain:

When the Lost Waif was returned to you as your son, whom you abandoned on the steps of the Madelaine in Paris, it was your duty to express your sincere appreciation to the nurse, Miss Beaton who was directed to bring me to you by the British Consul. At the time I could not speak the language but in the event you did not thank Miss Beaton, belatedly, I will do so in your behalf, provided you have found answers to the following.

I am not going to ask you, Mother dear, why you left me the way you did but I will ask you how in Hell could you do so, when, at the time you were in the Hartford Hospital in London?

If you were not a patient, then please state the reason you were not on the station platform in the company of the Inspector from Scotland Yard, when your son arrived. In any event, had you been there you would not have received him because it is quite evident that would be unlawful, as the results show two of his mothers were there but neither was given the opportunity to claim him.

Much publicity was given the boy prior to your being declared his mother. Strangely enough, not a word was printed after his arrival and his being taken into custody. Is it not most likely that after you're being declared the boy's mother that newspaper correspondents would hound you for your story concerning the abandonment of your son?

Did you have interests in Guatemala that you chose the Madelaine for the desertion? Or did you not know at the time that there is an exact replica of the edifice in the capital of that country? Regardless, the British Consulate should have told the Marines.

So, mother number three to the *Lost Waif*, I close with the hope that you sent sincere thanks to the prominent person or persons who were instrumental in effecting the reported reunion that did not take place, with one—the *Lost Waif*.

The Matron of the Hospital stated that the child did resemble the de Barrios from a picture shown to her by a Frenchman.

I am sincerely,

Lost Waif

Dear Mrs. Britton:

The Foreign Office reveals that you deserted your son, Edward Britton, in Paris on April 16th, 1904. Now, because the reports stating that I was found abandoned in Switzerland, not specifying which town or on what day and that the police in Dover state I was brought there on the 21st, it is assumed by the aforementioned Office that I could not be your son as he did not arrive in England until the 28th.

You are the number four Mother of the *Lost Waif,* whereas none (any mother) was found for me. Surely the officials could have spared one for me, instead of humiliating and degrading me to the level of a pauper.

That Office further states that your son was accompanied by a Miss Beaton but when the train pulled into Victoria Station she is nowhere to be seen or heard. The same goes for you.

Most sincerely,

No *Lost Waif* belonging to you.

Dear Señora Algerie Reyna de Barrios:

Throughout the years following the assassination of your husband and then the birth of your son, until the time he was found, I complement you for your courageous fortitude. Even though it is reported that you did this abandonment, you are to be admired for the way you kept him from being recognized for so long. It is apparent the authorities were determined to keep you separated from your son for good reasons-from their standpoint.

You were respected, perhaps feared, because of your knowledge of International Politics and also envied for your perpetuating enormous wealth. One portion of the wealth's source was overlooked, or rather, purposely never divulged.

During the Second World War, a group of people left America in search of quinine and discovered some in Guatemala, on a neglected plantation. They questioned the local inhabitants as to the ownership of that property. They were told, that the cinchona trees were planted by President General José Maria Reyna Barrios many years before. The discovery of quinine from the barks of these trees proved to be America's chief source of supply. Since then, though, science has improved on its' synthetic creation.

Regarding the beautiful house that was built and named for you, Algerie Ville, it still stands. English people have been occupying your home for over fifty years after you became the President's widow.

You used sound judgement in taking the steps you did but the obstacles were insurmountable. When just one statement from a British Consul saying that he discredits the story of Mrs. Turner is unquestionably believed. This includes the French, American and his own country's press. Yet he could not provide anything conclusive to substantiate his reasons other than telling the lie that he sent the boy to England to be reunited with you, his mother.

You lost your son at the same time that I lost my mother, each in similar circumstances that clearly indicates that you were mine and I, yours.

Although it is stated in the New Orleans paper that with the death of your supposed daughter she was the last of the Reyna de Barrios, rest assured it is not the case. You had a male offspring, he fathered one, added to him is another, so the line will yet carry on for a long time and with them this true story of untruths.

All that I write and have written is the result of the message that was given to me by the schoolmaster. He deprived me of recess to improve my writing when I was in the first grade. I was his only pupil, which now enables me at this time, to write at least one item from a newspaper that does not discredit you.

New York Tribune, August 5th, 1894 Mme. Reine de Barrios, wife of the President of Guatemala, has arrived by Pacific Mail Steam Ship at San Francisco, and will make a tour of this country. She has long been one of the leaders in Central American Society, and her influence has been powerfully felt in Central America Politics. She is a woman of more than ordinary perspicacity, and her advent into the social circles of American Society will introduce a new element, although Madame Barrios intends to return soon to that country which her husband has made so prosperous, Guatemala.

In that one paragraph, one can deduce the defamatory statements made regarding your behaviour-as being charged with drunkenness. Whereas you had been forcibly drugged, then one year later you were made to visit the child in the Convent, accompanied by a nurse while you were under the influence of drugs, so stated the Mother Superior.

Who is to doubt the words of such a devoted lady? At the time she believed Consuelo was your daughter because the person who brought you, said as much. At the same time Mother Superior admitted that she was not acquainted with the doings of the world outside yet she suspected foul play.

Regardless of the prestige, position or power a person may have, it proves to be an impossibility for that one person to commit a perfect crime, once an innocent and unquestionably, a truthful being, is used in the commitment of that crime.

These events took place more than the average life span ago but God has spared me. Perhaps for the purpose to remind those with such authority to be held in high esteem that they are not nearer to Him than those who have been suppressed, persecuted and robbed by such authorities. This was the case of the First Lady of Guatemala, Mme. Algerie Reyna de Barrios, my mother.

The lies are too numerous to prove otherwise, as told by the hierarchy. So that makes this hoax another wonder of the world: when a boy has four mothers. Yet I am raised as an orphan without having the opportunity to know any one of them.

All my love to you,

Joseph.

18

Guatemala After President Reyna Barrios

No greater honour could be bestowed on any statesman of a country than being the first ever to be elected by popular vote and then chosen to succeed himself, as was the case of General José Maria Reyna Barrios. This factor should warrant his being the subject of a biography, yet there is little more than two lines of printed words anywhere describing the qualifications of this man outside his country. No stone was left unturned to dispose of him and his beautiful, talented wife, their vast fortune and their son.

After his assassination, followed by the killing of his successor, (the First Vice-President) his supposed friend, family attorney and Second Vice-President, Cabrera, took over the Barrios wealth, properties and the reins of office. Needless to add, he did not just stop at confiscating the Barrios holdings. He began his reign of tyranny, gathering momentum throughout his two decades of vicious rule. He was a poor, struggling lawyer when, not then President Barrios, first met him and gave him his start by appointing him as trustee of his affairs-the family lawyer. Estrada Cabrera became the President by self-appointment when entering the Assembly with a pistol in his hand and thugs and made his declaration to that position, so the story goes. If this incident is not true, then the twenty-two years of his reign of terror proved it possible of his being capable of the act.

As an example, take the time when a new American Minister went to the Presidential Palace to present his credentials. Meanwhile a plot had been formulated among the cadets to kill the President because of his cruel ruling. It was arranged when the Minister was to make a public address. Somehow, at the last minute the President had got wind of it so he changed his plans for entering the Palace. He gave orders for the cadets to appear in the courtyard with unloaded rifles and without ammunition. One of them objected, he was placed under arrest and sometime later was shot.

The President, accompanied by two of his aides, arrived ahead of schedule by entering unexpectedly by a side door through a narrow passage. As he did so, the cadets who were lined up on either side, presented arms. Then the flag bearer lowered it so as to let it fall in the face of the President. He tried to brush it away with his hand. That gave the cue for the captain of the cadets to fire his pistol point blank at the President. However, the bullet stopped by his hand. One of his aides fired over the shoulder of the President, killing the captain of cadets, next another shot was fired killing the aide. Then the other aide, a German soldier of fortune, opened fire, killing two and wounding two others cadets.

The cadets did not retaliate probably on account of the confined quarters in fear of killing their own. Then a number of officers and soldiers rushed in and the cadets, some of whom were mere boys, scattered, panic stricken before the furious onslaught that ensued. As they ran through the Palace corridors, a half dozen more cadets were killed by pistols and sabers hired by the President.

When it was all over, it was found that the President was only slightly wounded. He was able to see the American Minister later in the day. He immediately conducted a personal investigation of this affair. It resulted in his having the captain of the cadets, also the flag bearer, executed in the Palace courtyard. It was discovered that three cadets had smuggled ammunition into their cartridge boxes but one had already been killed in the first attempt. The other two were shot the same day. The next day, the rest of the cadets were tried and shot dead in their barracks. They were all sons of the best families in Guatemala.

The entire corps of cadets were imprisoned and whipped with lashes between two and three hundred each, in order to extract confessions from them. Following that, the instructors, alumni and graduates of up to twelve years good standing were punished. While these cadets were being eliminated others were being treated in a like manner. Cadets who had been in prison, under suspicion for having plotted against the President a year earlier, when a bomb exploded under his carriage, killing one of the horses along with the coachman, were now executed, en masse. These latest victims were professionals; doctors, lawyers, and wealthy landowners. At another time, Cabrera's younger brother, also a Cadet, came to the Palace steps with several of his cadet friends to reason with his brother. These cadets were welcomed with bullets, ending all their lives.

Cadet bodies from several massacres were piled one on top of the other on an open cart pulled through the streets of the Capital, with the dependents and relatives followed, shrieking. The bodies were thrown into an open grave, unceremoniously. While these conditions existed there was no word or sign of an importation of a foreign assassin to liquidate this tyrant, therefore, it must have suited the persons who supported, financed, then double crossed Oscar Zollinger to kill the first President-Barrios-who was elected by the people. What a damn fool that killer was to ever think that he would live to collect that large sum of money, when the schemers of the plot would be known and risked being black-mailed!

Following the mass murders of well to do people, their properties were confis-cated and sold at auction to supposedly repay the government for the expenses incurred. Of course it was common knowledge that the Treasury Head was Cabrera who diligently guarded this department of his government. Within a short period of time afterwards, another two thousand Guatemalans were impris-oned. Among them were some delicate women who were brutally beaten and soon died from the effects. Fearing this treatment would be extended to others, many thousands fled the country into the adjoining countries and some were smuggled aboard ships to South America, United States and Europe. As many as more than thirty thousand people went to Mexico alone. The properties of all who fled were confiscated, regardless of the law in the country against such actions. The businesses, relatives and friends of those who fled were under close supervision and the selling of property or the transfer of mortgages was made impossible by lawyer-President Cabrera.

It so happened that at this time, the country's Minister of Foreign Affairs, an ignorant, uncouth half-breed Indian was the person to see before one could meet the President Cabrera. He held this position because the President needed his gutsy actions but in time Cabrera feared him more than any other person near him. That may have been the reason for Cabrera having German bodyguards who held high rank in his personal army. One of these bodyguards had been known to slash Indians with his sword if he did not get a salute from them. It became obvious that Cabrera's army was not loyal to him for the military posi-tion held, if it did not have some fringe benefits, such as a share in the spoils. But one bodyguard died by the cadets during the uprising in the Palace courtyard, thereby forfeiting his share.

The Foreign Minister, whose name, incidentally, was given as don Juan Bar-rios M., also had a reputation for being brutal. That may account for historians to mistakenly attach such a reputation to President José Reyna de Barrios. What the letter "M" means, remains a mystery and the Barrios genealogical tree gives no suspicious hint of him. But there is one explanation that comes to mind. Going back to when Justo Barrios became President, there had always been a Barrios member in government, although not necessarily the president. It was generally an on-going tradition that a Barrios in government would act as Guatemala's lucky charm because they had their personal wealth before entering politics and their name represented its own fair, trustworthy power amongst several continents. Justo's father migrated from Spain to marry his wife who was rooted to Guatemalan soil. He began to build on the family and his wealth through the sweat of his labours. No Barrios member turned away from helping others or supporting themselves. They were a united clan. They were all respected for their humility and compassion.

Such an example would be when Justo Barrios took his orphaned, begotten out of wedlock son into his heart and family. He educated this oldest son at America's West Point in New York, wanting to prime him to enter Guatemala's government.

Was Juan Barrios M using his real name? Did Cabrera carry on with country tradition in his own crude way?

Incidentally, the cadets who died by Cabrera's orders were educated in Guatemala's military academy, commonly referred to as the West Point of the South.

Due to the many attempts on the life of don Manuel Estrada Cabrera, he could not live in his private residence or his home in the suburbs but preferred to live in the heavily guarded Palace. His homes were occupied all the time with his spies and soldiers. This information came from one journalist who was allowed to interview Cabrera. Without any pretense or forethought, this interviewer drew the conclusion that Cabrera, like his predecessors, would die with his boots on.

Herein lies a big difference between him and one of his predecessors who was admired, along with his beautiful and talented American wife. Yet not doubting the fact that he did die with his boots on, nevertheless, it was not done by one of his countrymen. At the time that his life was being plotted against, President McKinley offered to send a warship to Guatemala to take Barrios out of the country but he refused. The previous year his brother was killed by an assassin without an apparent reason, probably by mistake, it was later assumed. Or was it to start trimming away on some Barrios tree branches?

At this time in Guatemala's history, Manuel Estrada Cabrera ruled the people his way but the country's finances was controlled by foreigners. This was the time when the United Fruit Company started by paying little, if anything, for thousands of banana acres. In fact, it had control of nearly all of Central America. Cabrera shook hands with these foreign investors. He needed their money to pay for his imported army so that he could be President. Then later he reneged on his word because he really did not like any foreigners.

Eventually, after twenty-two years of tyrannical rule, Estrada Cabrera was captured and placed in prison, than into an insane asylum. But during this reign of terror, another Barrios member was to lose his life. He was Antonio Barrios, the son of Justo and cousin of José. This happened during his trip to New York on one of the White Fleet, owned and operated by the United Fruit Company. The details concerning this matter are unattainable, such as the cause, date of death, name of the ship and it's position and the time of day. This was the untimely and mysterious end of the life of one who had graduated from the United States Military Academy, West Point.

In this instance, added to the others concerning the people who carried the name Barrios, it becomes apparent that it was an international unwritten law that such were not permitted to live free or if at all. Unfortunately we were unable to supply all answers when West Point contacted Josie in order to complete their records on Cadet Antonio Barrios.

When acts of this killing nature are performed or planned, by persons in positions of authority with the means at their disposal to have the treacherous deeds enacted, it results in nothing more than just being plainly reported in newspapers. However, on the other hand, when similar incidents of improper behaviour are done by the supposed lower class onto the upper class, then it becomes a totally different set of rules. Law enforcement departments are pressed into service, which in turn are funded by the taxpayers-the majority of whom are just the plain folk, all in the name of justice,

The true definition of justice is made to suit not the conditions but the persons involved, especially if they are of prominence. However, incidents of an uncommon nature may find their way into newspapers, although justice is not meted out in them, the newspapers contain the truth for the most part. For instance, the United Fruit Company issued a statement when inquiries were made requesting information regarding the death of Antonio Barrios, that their records were destroyed. On the other hand, the press reported the cause of death and the name of the ship but nothing further.

It is the likes of this kind of treatment of events as they are reported and recorded, that supplies material for stories. As an example, the *"Lost Waif"* is definitely a boy as the photo shows. Yet by British standards he is not Reyna de Barrios but at the same time it is a girl with the same name who is put into a convent in England. Of course, no newspaper in any country had a picture of Consuelo to print. Although somewhat contradictory, these revelations regarding the *Lost Waif* were exposed by the press, clearly showing that it was not the reporters who told the untruths.

At that time there were no direct lines of communication from Guatemala to the United States, also, the press was British controlled. Regardless of inconveniences, a strict censorship cannot suppress the news of all events that may be unfavourable to a country while there are travelers and truth seekers. I site the following examples for reference reminders.

BRITISH RECORDING AND REPORTING OR LACK OF SAME.

Within these pages has been revealed the gory events that took place on the night of April 23rd, 1918. Told by one (titled) person to the other one who wrote the glorified account of it some fifteen years later. Neither one was a participant. It is true that the first non-participant mentions the names of some who lost their lives. They were officers who said or did something brave before departing from this world. Beyond that, not one word is mentioned about an individual Tommie; such is the way history is recorded-just plain propaganda.

The titled one states that one part of the raid was concentrated on destroying the depot where submarines were being assembled. This is when and where some more lives were needlessly sacrificed because with the lock gates being rendered inoperative and the channel blocked, it would be a waste of time to build such vessels. A moot explanation.

When this day-dedicated to Saint George-comes each year, it is then that I bow my head in prayer for those lives. Not one unknown, but at least eight hundred twenty-one men unknown to me, were slaughtered to benefit an ego of the naval perpetrator of these crimes. It is on this day that three simple words cross my mind, as the tears stream down my face in memory of those unfortunate men, "Lest We Forget."

Another incident of the glorification of an event happened on the H.M.S. James Fletcher when it rammed the submarine. This was nothing more than an accident. At night the commander would leave the patrol area to be near Dover, then when dawn came, would return. One night there was only one man at the wheel who served as the lookout too, with no officer of the watch. The ship was steaming slowly without navigation lights when it struck an object that was submerged. The ship bounced back and struck the object again. After the first collision, voices could be heard that were not in English, so the report of sinking the submarine went like this:

The commander got a call from the bridge that a submarine had been sighted, whereupon he issued the order to give chase at full speed, although it meant leaving his patrol, eventually catching up to her and ramming her.

This seems plausible enough, yet the Commander did not send a wireless message to Dover or seek assistance in the chase from any of the numerous vessels in the vicinity. Then again, he was chasing a vessel that had at least twice the speed of his own and the damage inflicted as the result of the collision was nothing more than a slight disfigurement of the stem post that did not call for any repairs to be made. She also went for the next three years or until she returned to her owners in this condition. So, an enemy ship had been sunk through an act of presence of mind and bravery or by a stroke of dumb luck. The way it was recorded and reported by those with authority received priority.

From the incident, the top brains did not come to the conclusion that the enemy submarines were using commercial shipping lanes to return to their home bases. That called for all merchant ships to just travel by day and only in this theatre of war.

Going back to that day of February of 1896, when a British subject shot the President of Guatemala, there is not a word of it to be found in the English Press. The same applies to the finding of the *Lost Waif.* The French Press gave that incident extensive coverage. One American paper in that country reported it. Just one English paper gave a somewhat distorted version, conceding to the French for its news. The cables to America were under British control, so, there again, nothing was reported to the United States or Canada-that was also British controlled. Since all news regarding that event ceased from the moment that the Inspector from Scotland Yard took that boy from his Mother and with my not being an atheist, I thank God that repercussions have not visited me. It's been over fifty years and yes, I do count them.

Shortly after making a legal entry into this country, for the sake of passing time I went into a movie theatre with no special interest. What came on that screen most certainly drew my attention. The feature was titled, "Five Came Back," starring a renowned English actor. In the cast was a small boy being transported on the plane in the custody of a detective. At intervals in the showing, the camera was brought to focus on billboards at an airport depicting scenes with the one word on the top of each, GUATEMALA. This picture was made from the novel of the same name but as of this day I have not been fortunate enough to obtain it. Could this be called coincidence? That author, if he is lucky enough to get to read this, will then know what followed after the detective made his delivery.

It was about six years later after this movie showed that the big, brave inspector who was strong enough to wrest the boy from the arms of a heart-broken mother on the platform of the railway station, that he wrote his memoirs for consumption in this country. In there is not one word of his noble deed. Had it been too much for him to live with? Could it be that at the time he was married, possibly with a child and could do this deed without a feeling of guilt? It is assumed that by his wearing a boutonnière was for the purpose of the imposters to be able to recognize him but the unexpected appearance of the real mother and nurse may have thrown him off guard, that when the moment of decision came, he took with him neither of the cheats but the boy's nurse.

It most certainly would have been manly, had he also taken the mother with him. It would have vindicated himself yet still have obeyed orders. Furthermore, it would have made better sense. One can see why he could not take the boy accompanied by Mrs. Turner. She had reported to the Metropolitan Police that the boy was the son of the assassinated President of Guatemala and that she had been his nurse for a year. This raises the question as to why it was she who went with the Inspector alone and not with the woman who had brought the boy from France? Could it be because she would have dispelled the whole conspiracy if allowed her freedom? What about the woman who traveled with the boy from France? There is no mention of her even stepping from the train, yet according to the British Consul she was from the British Charities. Conspiracy begins with the same letter of the alphabet. The news reporter does state that he knew the Detector-Inspector. Could friendship have over-ruled good judgment in his reporting the train depot incident?

If the treatment I received during my incarceration is the British idea of charity, then I am grateful to God that He has protected me for this length of time. I am now enabled not only to tell this story but to write it and to prove to the editor of whom it subsequently will be requested to published it, that there is not a trace of senility of my mentality due to age.

According to the law of averages, I should have long since been dead but it has been my purpose for many years to expose these events truthfully when those involved with the treachery have long since gone and fortunately it has been accomplished thus far.

During the year of 1938 I was stricken with acute-arthritis from my head down to my feet, requiring my being hospitalized for four months where I was placed in the hands of a delicate young doctor who was serving his internship. He gave me hope when he told me that it can be cured but it will take time. I was transported to surgery, to use his term, he had my tonsils "Yanked out" along with some teeth. For a year following surgery the condition gradually cleared then for the next eight years I was free of that condition. Then it reoccurred. After two months in a hospital I had to leave to make a legal re-entry into America. One more attack of it came six years later but of short duration.

Now for the so-called British Charities' representative who had no intention of seeing that right would be done. Although the Consul in Paris issued the statement to the French press that the boy was being taken to his mother, this "charitable" person knew otherwise and did nothing.

If, during the writing of the Inspector's memoirs, did this incident slip his memory or was it that he acted on orders, once again not to mention it? In the first instance it is very doubtful yet the second is more logical.

Now compare the two reported incidents of the abandonment of these boys who are dressed identically. Neither boy is speaking English but the one brought, supposedly, from Switzerland is placed in the hands of a detective to deliver to the Police in Dover but the *Lost Waif* is claimed by the British Consul; given to a woman to bring to England and she leaves him on a railway station to be picked up by another person. I cannot find it in me to classify him as a man, wearing the flower in his lapel, pre-arranged for her benefit, too.

The same Consul was knighted. It may have been because he distinguished himself by winning a legal victory when he represented a Danish shipping company. One of its vessels had been involved in a collision with an American ship. That still did not win the States back.

Now, many years have passed since all the happenings referred to and some changes have been made. The land acquired from Guatemala in the middle of the nineteenth century that became known as British Honduras, has in recent years been made independent, with the name being changed to that of the capital city Belize (also spelled, Belicè), following the example set by the country that did and should own it.

Many years ago there was a distinct difference between the two capital cities-Guatemala City being the cleanest city in the world, while Belize, so reported by an Englishman who paid a visit there, was the filthiest. Maybe under that existing rule, the people had to make do what the seamen of that nation were required to do with one pail of water each day? I have since learned that Belize has greatly improved its image.

To whom should I express my sincere gratitude for having survived nearly four score years to be able yet to accomplish this writing task? Primarily; I owe it to England, for making it so intolerable to exist in my circumstances that I developed an anxious desire to leave that country and never to return. Although it may be their wish that I did return as they would make such arrangements even though I was never a citizen of that country. As of yet I have not put in a claim for it, but that country is indebted to me in the sum of two pounds, from December 31, 1926. With interest applied, that should total a little tidy amount after fifty-two years.

In 1921 I joined the Royal Naval Reserve, not for patriotic reasons but that I would be able to get a job as a seaman on the merchant ships. On some ships, it is a requirement, especially on the large passenger ships. In order to join, one had to be a British subject. I am now in possession of an affidavit stating that I was not. Although I jumped a ship after serving the five years enlistment time, I now have a lien against England.

Secondarily; these United States was then and it is still the best country in the world. It is especially so for me when I was able to come in the middle of winter, to get a job that enabled me to exist. Although it was menial work, I was in much better circumstances than ever I had experienced before. There are unbounded opportunities for everyone in this land. Also, I give thanks for the recovery of my health due to the treatment afforded my wife and me at very little cost. I give thanks that at this late stage in life I am well enough even now to swim a mile, non-stop and in free style. It is something I learned to do from one of this country's leading swimmers who was so renowned for his acting in a series of jungle films. I speak of Johnny Weissmuller who played Tarzan. But I did not copy his famous yell.

I have done this free style swimming for a worthy charity, to express my appreciation and enabling me to use common sense enough to stop smoking after forty-eight years. In turn it allows that I may accomplish this act (swimming) that gives me great pleasure to do.

There is One to whom I owe the greatest debt of gratitude for not only keeping me here but for the protection He gave when I did foolish things-some times unconsciously and especially so, for not having me included that day in that huge floating grave that lay so near to me for one week. I am grateful to the H.M.S. Vindictive, for missing that floating mine in the first hour of service to a country that kicked me to one side after having use of my mother and me and especially during my escapades on that unruly trawler, the S.T.Cevic.

In this regard I feel that I have received Your full blessings and my closing prayer is for the many orphans throughout the world, "Please Father in Heaven, protect and guide them all as you have done for me, Amen."

GLOSSARY

Action Station	Center of communications, receiving and sending messages/orders
Aerial bomb	Aircraft dropping bombs
After gallast sheave	A pulley for gathering in a sail.
Almshouse	Poor house
Amidship	Midway between the bow and the stern.
Amongst	Also among-surrounding
Astern	To the rear of a vessel.
Australasia	Islands of Oceania in the South Pacific, including Australia, New Zealand, New Guinea and associated islands.
Ballasted	Any heavy material placed in the hold to assist stability.
Barrage Patrol	One or more ships acting as an obstruction in a watercourse.
Battle of Jutland	The only major naval battle between England and Germany in 1916, fought about 70 miles west of Jutland, which is a peninsula of northern Europe.
Battle of Trafalgar	A cape on the Atlantic coast of southern Spain where in 1805 Nelson defeated the French and Spanish fleets in a naval battle.
Bilges	Lowest inner parts of a ship's hull, where water collects.
Bird	Slang for worthless due to drinking grog.
Bitch of the Sea	Slang for the vessel.
Bloke	Slang for fellow or man.
Blotter-pad habit	Drinking
Bobbies	Policemen

Bollard	Thick post for securing ropes and hawsers.
Boulogne–sur-Mer (full name)	Seaport on northern coast of France and on the English Channel.
Bowline	The rope leading forward from the leech of a square sail to hold the leech forward when sailing close-hauled.
Breakwater	A barrier protecting a shore or harbor from full impact of waves.
Brew	Ale or beer.
Brogue	Strong dialect accent.
Bullybeef	Canned pickled beef
Bunkers	Bins or tanks for fuel storage.
Bunting tosser	Nickname for signal-boy because the flags he uses are made from light, bright cotton materials.
Cannon fodder	Servicemen considered to be expendable materials of war.
Cape Griz Nez	Promontory of northern France, extending into the Strait of Dover.
Channel raiders	Coined name for the ships in the Dover Channel looking for enemy ships or subs.
Cheeky	Mischievous.
Cheque	Check.
Chuffed	Happy.
Cockney	A native of the East End of London.
Constables	policemen
Cordite	A smokeless explosive powder extruded in cords.
Coxswain	A person who steers the boat.
Cricket	Outdoor British game played with bats, balls and wickets.
Crystal Palace	Populat London theater.
Cutter	A mainsail, and two or more headsails which are usually set flying.
Davy Jones's locker	The grave of all who die at sea.
Ditty bag	Sailor's bag to carry small items.

Doldrums	A period of inactivity.
Dover Union	Workhouse in Dover, England.
Downs	An expanse of rolling, grassy upland in southern England.
Drifter patrol	One or more ships perusing the channels.
Epsom salts	A cathartic
Eton collar	White broad collar
Faroe Islands or Faeroe Islands	Group of Danish islands in the North Atlantic Ocean, between the Shetlands and Iceland.
Farthing	One quarter penny
Fidley	Tight nook usually in remote corner of a ship.
First Sea Lord	Admiral
Flagship	Vessel leading a fleet bearing the flag.
Flotilla	Group of ships resembling a fleet.
Forecastle or fo'c's'le	Section of the upper deck of a ship, located at the bow and forward of the foremast.
Forenoon	Daylight morning hours between sunrise and noon.
Fore-side	Front or upper side.
Fortnight	14 days and nights or 2 weeks.
Goodwin Sands	Ten miles of shoals in the Strait of Dover.
Goodwin Sands Lightship	Lighthouse.
Grog	Alcoholic liquor, especially rum diluted with water.
Guinea	Equaled one pound, one shilling
Guy Fawkes Day	A gun powder plot to assassinate the king, 1605.
Half crown	Two shillings and six pence
Half pence	Half penny–pronounced "hay penny"
Halyards	Ropes used to raise or lower a sail or flag.
Harry Tates' Navy	British comedian
Hatch batten	Piece of wood used to secure an opening leading to the hold.

Headmaster	The workhouse administrator.
Heave	To hoist or throw.
Hell Wagons	Slang for the fighting British vessels.
Helmsman	One who steers the ship.
Husband	Master of the ship.
Ignorant fishermen	Slang for men who fished aboard ships close to land.
Isle of Man	British island in the Irish Sea.
Jack Johnson	Boxer.
John Bull	Typical Englishman.
Jonah	A person who is thought to bring bad luck.
Kebles	A small piece of wood used to keep the mesh gauge equally uniform.
Ketch or catch or cache	Two-masted fore-and-aft rigged sailing vessel with a mizzen or a jigger mast stepped aft of a taller mainmast that is forward of the rudder.
Lather boy	Barber's apprentice.
Lee	The side sheltered from the wind.
Lockdoors	When the trawl is thrown out but does not properly open to collect the fishes. It folds over on itself.
Mal-de-mer	Seasickness
Mangold wurzels	Football sized turnips
Mine-layers	The ships assigned to planting mines on the ocean floor.
Mosquito Fleet	One or more PT boats.
Mufti	Civilian dress.
Nine-point-two	Cathartic
Ofttimes	Also often times-frequently.
One pound (after 1971)	One hundred new pence
Ostende also Ostend	Seaport on the North Sea in northwestern Belgium.
Paddle minesweeper	Ship propelled by wheels assigned to search for mines.
Page	Boy employed in a hotel to run errands and carry messages.

Paupers' Palace	Slang name for workhouse.
Pence	Similar to our penny
Penury	Extreme poverty.
Pick-a-back	Piggyback
Poaching	Fishing in a forbidden area.
Pompom	A large machine gun firing one pound shells.
Poorhouse	A place where paupers are interred.
Porpoises	Gregarious aquatic mammals such as dolphins.
Port	Left hand side of a ship facing forward.
Port quarter	Area located on the left-hand side of the ship.
Pound sterling	British monetary system, currency changed in February 15, 1971 * except the pound.
Programme	Program
Prohibition	U.S. law (1920-1933) forbidding all alcoholic beverages to be manufactured, transported, sold and consumed.
Publican	Tavern keeper or tax collector.
Quay	A wharf.
Quay	Wharf.
Quid	British slang for pound sterling.
Quinine	Used to treat malaria, derived from the bark of the cinchona tree of Guatemala.
Rounder	Game similar to baseball.
Rove	Past tense of reeve, to fasten through or around.
Salford	City in southeastern Lancashire.
Salvoes	Simultaneous discharge of firearms.
Schoolmaster	Principle of British school
Scottisches	Scottish melodies.
Semaphore	Visual signaling by flags, lights or moving the arms.
Shanghai	To kidnap for compulsory service aboard a ship.

Shilling	Twenty shillings equaled one pound sterling
Shoal	A sandy elevation in the sea water making a shallow depth.
Sinecure	A commission or charge requiring no work and provides a compensation.
Smack	A sloop-rigged boat used for commercial fishing.
Snobbye	British shoemaker
Soused	Drunkard
Splash	Act of warfare.
Spuds	Slang for potatoes.
Starboard	Right-hand side of a ship.
Starboard	Right hand side of a ship facing forward.
Strait	Narrow passage of water connecting two larger bodies of water.
Suds	Slang for beer.
Ta, la ta	Thank you, goodbye.
Taube	German plane carrying bombs
Teetotalers	Non-drinkers of all alcoholic beverages.
Telegraphist	Telegrapher
Tip cat	Game to unbalance your opponent.
Tommies	Slang for British soldiers.
Tot	A small amount of liquor.
Tram-car	Street car.
Twin-screw ship	Having two propellers, one on either side of the keel, that usually revolve in opposite directions.
Union Jack	Flag of the United Kingdom.
Webley Colt	Type of revolver.
Whence	From what source or origin.
White cliffs of Dover	The appearance of white cliffs due to the lime (chalky) deposits of the earth.

Workhouse	Former British public institution in which the indigent were fed and forced to work.
Yacht patrol	One or more ships capable to cruise or run the waters with more speed and efficiency than other types of ships.
Yardarm	Either end of a yard of a square sail.
Yeomanry	Volunteer cavalry force organized in 1761 to serve as a home guard and later incorporated into the British Army.
Zeebrugge	Town in northwestern Belgium, the port for Bruges.

0-595-31341-8

www.ingramcontent.com/pod-product-compliance
Lightning Source LLC
Chambersburg PA
CBHW020916290526
45784CB00002BA/572